SHAFTS *of* GOLD

Faye Roots

Published in the United States of America

ISBN 979-8-9924880-4-3 (SC)

ISBN 979-8-9924880-8-1 (HC)

ISBN 979-8-9924880-9-8 (Ebook)

For Book Rights Adaption and other Rights Permission.

Call us at toll-free **601-914-6178**.

Table of Contents

Intro to *Shafts*

This is the memoir of a shy girl and her search for the *right* path for her life. It is also the story of an extraordinary God and shafts of gold which sometimes broke through to guide the child – and then the young woman – on her life's journey.

CHAPTER 1

Early Years — A Seed Sprouts

I, Faye Tognola, was born during the Second World War years of the twentieth century.

In June 1943, my father was fighting overseas. His family did not know where; they were told the Middle East. This was true in the beginning, but in the final few years of his military life, he served in the jungles of Papua New Guinea.

He came home only twice in seven years and did not meet me until the end of 1946. My mother told me years later that I terrified him – a gentle, trusting hazel-eyed blonde little girl, so different to where he had been and what he had suffered. My 3-year-old self must have been a shock. He was a loving husband and father, but there was a distance between us that lasted until the final years of his life.

My mother and my half-sister, Maureen, were my early nurturers, but the thirteen-year age difference between my sister and myself meant that she was married and left our home when I was still incredibly young. Memories of those times are now shadowy. I only know I was loved, cared for, and protected. My sister's intervention indeed protected me from harm from older girls and their attempts to influence me when I started school. Maureen saw something when she passed the school, told my mum. Only I ever knew what harm was averted, and I was never able to say, 'Thank you, big sister.'

One of my earliest clear memories in my life is of a stretch of sandy beach and rolling waves. A huge building with holes in the walls on the front and sides loomed over everything. My grandmother, for a few short years, owned a beach house on Bribie Island, off the coast of Queensland, Australia. Mum, Maureen, and I visited. This was the only time I remember when we ever visited her there. It was necessary to come on a boat. My mum and I both became seasick.

I was young, around 3 years old. My dad came home at the end of the same year. It was probably 1946. My nan spoke seriously to me that day. Most of what she said, I cannot remember, but she spoke of the war. She told me to remember the building on the sand with the holes for cannons that guarded the island. She also spoke that day gently to me of love and loss and held me tightly and told me to walk the 'right' path.

I am grateful for this grandmother, although I did not at all understand why her spirituality often seemed to worry my dad in the next few short years. She was from a strongly Celtic Scottish background and had married a strict Presbyterian miner who ruled his family – wife Nan and my mum and her three siblings – with a rod of iron. He was the head of the family, and hellfire awaited all who did not live by his rules. I think this was why when he died quite young, long before I was born, my nan escaped like a bird and flew into some very strange spiritual areas. She was known as a clever teacup reader and dabbled in fortune telling in the tea rooms and café she owned.

My mother once told me seriously, 'You are very like your nan, but you must find your own path. Remember always that *imagination is a gift, but a lie is wrong and a distortion of truth. There is no such thing as a "white" lie.'*

This single piece of information was vital to me as I walked my own pathway of spiritual discovery. I remember looking upwards with a kind of heartfelt longing and prayer. *Help me to find the right way.*

I loved my schooldays but, as a painfully shy child, suffered much from being 'misunderstood' or overlooked. I remember my first week of school with sadness. I twice wet my pants and had to endure hearing how frustrated the teachers were that I came to school before I turned 5 – bright enough to be accepted but *not* toilet trained. It was not until someone, perhaps my mum, explained that I could not draw attention to myself by putting up my hand and asking to go that I was allowed to quietly exit when necessary, and the problem never occurred again.

This became the pattern for early school life. I was not selected for plays, participation in sports, or classroom discussions because of my quiet, settled manner. I desperately wanted to put myself forward but was too self-conscious.

One memorable event at school happened when my class was selected to perform in the pantomime *Snow White* at a local hall. Oh, how much I wanted a part! My classmates leapt around – 'Pick me! Pick me!' – and children tried out for various roles. I sat quietly. At the close of the selection session, someone noticed me. I was quietly invited to be an understudy for the wicked queen. *I was delighted.*

My class teacher was surprised. He said later, 'Why didn't you tell me you were interested?'

I went to every rehearsal. I learned the lines and felt all the drama and passion. I began to understand at this time of my journey that I could do anything if I hid behind the costume of a different person. Being personally invisible became my goal.

This was confirmed to teachers when the unexpected occurred. The girl who had the part of the queen tearfully announced that she could not do it. They intended to blacken her teeth and wanted her to act really evil. It was two days before the opening, and she refused to do her part. I heard a lot of discussion about whether the play should be cancelled.

I walked up to a teacher and, with confidence, said, 'I have been rehearsing. I know the lines. I can *do this*.'

My first time before the eisteddfod in the hall, I surprised everyone, including myself, with how much I became involved in the character of that evil queen. On the night in the hall, my parents were frightened for me, but I discovered that if Faye were lost behind the costume and even the blackened teeth, I could *become* someone else.

Our school won the eisteddfod that year – certainly not because of me, but I did get a mention in the paper. 'A fine portrayal of the wicked queen by Faye Tognola – congratulations! Your strong Australian accent will be improved by speech training and elocution.'

My very Aussie father was furious. 'What's the matter with an Aussie accent?' he shouted.

I was not at all upset by the comment. The queen came 'alive'; that was nothing to do with Faye, the person.

My most valuable lesson occurred when I was 8. I went to church with my parents; it was the first time since my sister's wedding. I remember it was for a funeral. Some distant cousin had died.

I sat in that gloomy, dark brown church, feeling bored as adults spoke on and on. What they were saying meant nothing to me. I tried to be patient and still – but then I saw something.

I <u>saw</u> something that triggered a hunger in me to seek after what was true and Holy. The dark dusty corner of that church was infused suddenly with a bright light, and I saw figures with human likeness and wings with hands clasped as if in prayer.

It was so breathtakingly beautiful, I called out, 'Look! Look up there! They must be angels. They're saying prayers.' I pointed empathically.

My voice echoed in that large building. Faces automatically turned towards the dark corner.

My mother muttered, 'Oh, shush, darling.'

A woman across the aisle said, 'What a dear little child – and what a vivid imagination she must have.'

I learnt a life lesson that day. I would never again tell grownups what I, as a child, could see. The time at that church service changed my way of thinking. I sat looking up into that corner, focussed on something that was *real* and beautiful. I longed to know more.

On the way home, my dear mother hugged me and said, 'I know you saw something, darling. Your face was radiant.' She added, 'It was such a boring service. Maybe old Fred needed lots of praying people to travel with him.'

CHAPTER 2

Sprouting Years

I had no idea that my personal life and my spiritual life were in such an intrinsic tangle. I will try to unravel them, to share as normal life events unfolded. Perhaps the God shafts will become clearer as the written is recorded.

My childhood years were prominently happy ones. When my sister married, I was her flower girl. In a pretty blue dress with flowers in my hair, I was a *flower girl*. This was the year I started school as a prep child. This was once the introduction to primary school life and began with the basics. It was expected when we started 'big school' in our 6th year of life that we would be able to write, know our alphabet, and be mature in areas of polite behaviour and dealing with other students. Also, by the end of this prep year, I had got over my terror of putting up my hand. In the ways of childhood, I felt I was progressing OK.

My only hiccup this year that I can recall came when I was dressed like an angel for a Christmas concert. I had only four words to say, and then I was to walk off the stage slowly and daintily. The words were 'I see a light'.

Happily, I skipped onto the stage platform and piously folded my hands. I raised my eyes and saw a sea of faces looking at me from the darkness. I *froze*. I then burst into sobbing tears and had to be scooped off the stage with a very un-angelic lack of beauty and dignity.

'She will certainly not be a public speaker,' a voice said from the darkness. A few folk softly chuckled.

My future years would prove differently. I learnt a lesson. If you, as a person, can be hidden, you can do lots. However, hiding was safer. That is why my success in *Snow White* a few years later was significant; I was hidden by the wicked queen. The year of my 6th birthday stands out strongly in my memories for many reasons.

I Started Big School.

I felt grown up. This growing up was confirmed later in the year when my baby brother was born. I was now a *big sister*. I loved my little brother passionately and protectively. I even prayed to Someone I had been taught was 'out there'. I asked Him to give my brother a long life. *Please let him live till he is 30.* (That seemed a great age and was as far as I could count.)

A note of reflection: the year my brother turned 30 was, for me, a year of gentle concern. I knew more about God by then but still worried that maybe I had spiritually put a cloud over his life. Superstition and faith and God's gifts need much unravelling, and this was – and is – the story to find my truth in it *all*. I did enjoy his 31st birthday with relief and joy.

After John's birth in November, it seems Christmastime came suddenly. This year, a baby born in a stable made more sense. I knew what a baby meant to a family. I knew why everyone was happy. What I did not understand was a song we were told to sing at school. It was called 'Away in a Manger'. The teachers smiled; the children clapped. I stood at the back with tears running down my face. I thought it was one of the saddest songs I had ever been taught.

When I told my mum, she laughed. She hugged me as she carefully explained that I had got some words and the interpretation wrong. My dad, at that time, was working with a road maintenance crew, and each day, he went off to work with his 'crib', i.e. lunch in a crib box, i.e. lunch box.

My song line was sad. 'Away in a manger, no crib for a bear.' A new-born baby in a horse stable with no food, not even enough for a bear. Sad! So sad!

That Christmas, the story was told to me, and the beauty I found has never been lost. It stays with me today. While I was told that the baby was a special baby born for a *special reason*, it took many years of personal journeying to find for myself the *truth* of *who* this long-ago baby actually was and the man H became and *is* – even *today*.

***

In February the next year, when my brother was only six weeks old, my sister had her first child. I became an *aunt*, and my tiny brother became *Uncle* John. All this was amazing to me. I was still only 6 years old!

***

The year I turned 11 is full of many clear memories for me.

Both my grandmothers unexpectedly died – One far away whom I had only met once and my nan, who was close. One of my last conversations with my nan was her certainty that she had 'seen' her long-gone little girl – my mother's little sister who died at age 11 from health complications and diabetes.

'I'll be seeing her again soon,' she said.

That was the last time I saw nan. She died in a care home not long after. 'Where have my grandmothers gone?'

My parents said, 'They are now both at rest.'

Billy Graham the evangelist was in Australia that year, and his message seemed clear: 'Make a choice. Follow Jesus or go to hell.'

I remember clearly that I stood up and, in my heart, said, 'Yes! I will follow Him.'

Not long after, another street evangelist said, 'You must be baptised. You need to be fully immersed.'

My parents raised no objections when I was baptised this way. My heart was in the event, and I remember it was joyful and peaceful, but I had no clear evidence of personal change or confidence. No one followed up on me, and life settled back into ordinary daily struggles and achievements.

As a family, we did not go regularly to church. My dad once told a Catholic priest he had been a Salvation Army person since the war. He told the Salvos, when they came round, that he was a Catholic. That stopped them visiting.

We always had a special remembrance of Jesus at Christmastime and also at Easter. We had Christmas fun and Easter eggs at Easter but always, always this awareness that it was a remembrance of something more serious.

'He is important. You and your brother must find you own way.' My father's words resonate to this day.

I certainly journeyed down many diverse paths until I found my way. I won an essay competition and, during this 11th year of life, marched with the Salvos behind a band, joined a youth group, and grew up. I found in writing great personal satisfaction. I spent hours writing a journal not about my life but always expressing imagination fuelled by the things around me. I never actually *saw* anything after the angels in the church when I was 8, but somewhere as well as imagination, I knew there was more beyond the world we lived in. Who? What? How?

So my life journey continued.

CHAPTER 3

Maturing and Learning

Before my 13th birthday, another event occurred which shocked my parents. The clarity and certainty disturbed me.

I had a dream. I was playing tennis. The ball was hit and flew high into the air. It landed. *Thud!* The asphalt surface of the tennis court reverberated. The sound woke me up.

Then I heard water rushing, rushing, just like when the ocean tide was going out. My small bedside clock clearly gleamed in the darkness – 2:00 a.m. I *knew* – I *knew!* – someone known to us had just died. I told my parents.

They responded kindly, 'It's only a dream, love. Forget all about it.'

I tried, yet in my heart, I *knew* it was true. I also sensed it was not meant to cause *fear* but to 'prepare'. I found it hard to settle.

The policeman came in midmorning. He had a piece of torn paper in his hand. A man walking along the main road after his car had apparently broken down was killed by a 'hit-run' driver. His smashed wristwatch showed the time of impact at 2:00 a.m. The piece of paper was the only identification in the dead man's pocket. It had my father's name and address on it.

Dad, with a strange *peace* in his heart (he later told me), returned to the accident site with the officer and then accompanied him to the morgue to identify the body of a dear friend. This *peace* lasted with Dad as he later comforted Rick's grieving widow and children.

It was a powerful incident in my family's life but certainly impacted me profoundly. Was God of influence in the spirit world? Who indeed is *H*?

***

Years passed, and I grew up. Life continued to swirl in many directions. I loved learning, and primary and secondary school melded together. A small ear One boy died at primary school when hit by a car. Sadness impacted us all. He was only 5. Why? Where did he go?

At high school, one of the seniors was murdered by her ballet partner, who then killed himself. He left a letter: 'I loved her so much, I never wanted to lose her.' His parents, her parents, everyone who knew her asked the question 'Why?' I was filled with regret because I had watched the beauty of her grace and talent and felt like a nothing in comparison. She was only 16, and he was 18. Why? Where was God? They both went to church and attended youth groups.

I remained a rather shy, background person. when my maths teacher in high school asked me if I would be prepared to nurture and lead a small Sunday School class in the little Anglican church down the road from where my family now lived. He never asked me if I was an Anglican or what I believed but simply said that these eight little ones needed me. I said yes.

I learned much about the Christian faith during the two years with those children. The teaching manual was informative. I loved the children, and they loved me. The church folk never asked me for my credentials. They showed me love and appreciation, and this was my first experience of being part of a *church family*.

***

I asked a lot of questions in my younger years of the leaders in Christian ministry. All were extremely helpful, but no one seemed to want to discuss my queries about the unseen spirit world. No one in my memory ever taught about the trinitarian part of God's identity, but I was told to 'follow Jesus and accept by faith that God is three in *one* God – *trinity*'.

My belief in Jesus was strong as I grew up, but it was implied as a 'lack of faith' if we did not simply accept but kept questioning. I'm grateful, looking back today, that what I have learned and experienced personally has made my faith today not about another religion among others but about a relationship with a God so vast whose Love is so *profound*, it has no equal. There is only one *way* to eternity. My childhood rapidly passed as the story continues.

CHAPTER 4

Maturing Physically

Questioning Mentally and Spiritually

I left school before my 16th birthday and graduated from high school with full secretarial qualifications. The totally unexpected happened. I was offered a job in the city of Brisbane as a staff member on the leading daily newspaper of the day, he *Courier Mail*. Maybe, just maybe, I would one day be a reporter on that paper, i.e. a journalist. To be a writer was a deep longing in my heart.

I was delighted to accept a position as a copy girl and, for eight and a half years, loved the excitement of a city newspaper's hectic life. I loved all aspects of this life and gratefully accepted any opportunities to expand my own life in the process. The staff were encouraged to participate in providing community help in many and diverse areas. Financial assistance was offered by the newspaper to help defray costs if salary was lost on training days.

With the prompting of a cousin, I joined the Citizens Military Army (CMF) as a member of the Women's Army Corp, training in Signals. I learnt about Morse code and all areas of military signaling etc. Most machines, like teleprinters and Morse, are now redundant, but early radar has now progressed beyond early comprehension. Much training and knowledge gleaned by 'weekend warriors' was necessary for training and is probably still classified under the Official Military Secrets Act.

This period of my life was exciting and expansive. I learnt a lot about discipline, self-control, and living under difficult conditions in the army. I knew about loyalty and duty to God, Queen, and country. I learnt about rushing about each day to meet deadlines at the newspaper, but spiritually, it was a quiet, laid-back season, where God was not really thought about at all.

Then towards the end of my 18th year of life, I attended a rodeo in a country town. What happened on the way home made me really think about life and its meaning. In the next three years, I travelled on a coach trip to Central Australia and stayed in New Zealand. These *three* events, I will describe in the following chapter. Together, they made me acutely aware that I had a deep sensitivity to spiritual things, and I desperately needed to cement my personal *truth*.

***

One event of world-shattering impact occurred while I was at the *Courier Mail*. In 1963, November, Pres John F. Kennedy was assassinated. I was working on the Saturday morning when the news broke worldwide. Every teleprinter in the room began to disgorge pages of information, from journalists and newspapers in every corner of the globe. Usually, my job was to take the paper info from the teleprinter and carefully cut each item and put it on the desk for the relevant journalist to read, i.e. fishing reports – weather events to the sub-editor for his daily column and sometimes reams of court reports, police reports, and political stuff. What could I do about this?

All thirty-nine teleprinters were churning out an endless supply of questions – info and stories etc., all with one subject: the unbelievable *shock* of the Kennedy murder. Fortunately, a team of journalists were called in by the editor, and it took the whole day and into the night before all the information had been read and sorted.

I will surely not forget 22 November 1963 – my brother's 14th birthday!

CHAPTER 5

Figure on the Road

This is a true life happening, but I wrote it as a short story because its effect had such an impact on my life, I could not simply write it as a diary entry. Is God more, so much more, than just the biblical person revealed as the man Jesus Christ? What about the shining beings I saw when I was a little girl? Questions would gradually have answers, but there was a lot of life to be lived first.

Figure on the Road

I was 18 years old.

'You're driving too fast! Please slow down!'

My friend's cry from the front seat jolted me to full awareness. Stately gum trees lined the red ribbon country road and blurred into white flashes as the small car sped past. The moon shimmered with drifting haze and bathed the road with golden light.

We were travelling very fast. *How foolish to have accepted a lift home with two friendly cowboys from the country rodeo.* Their suggested visit to the lookout seemed now a dangerous detour. My companion slumped, apparently asleep, on the back seat beside me. His cowboy hat had fallen to the floor.

'Please don't drive so fast.' My voice was firm, but I hoped it sounded friendly and didn't betray the rising panic I was feeling.

The driver laughed. 'It's a glorious evening. Look at the open road. Not a car in sight. It's good to be alive!' He began to sing, 'We're just rollin' along, singing a song' as he pushed his foot even harder on the accelerator.

The light sedan swayed as the wheels hummed along the russet surface. It felt a bit like flying.

Then I saw something. It was in the distance, a vague shape – but becoming larger and more distinct. It was in the middle of the road. I leaned across the seat to get a clearer view.

A figure – was it a human figure? Washed by moonlight, the shape had form but no obvious indication of gender. Its clothing seemed to float from shoulder level and disappeared onto the red road. Flanked by the ghost gums, it stood perfectly straight and still.

'There's someone on the road. Slow down! Slow down!' My cry startled the driver.

He turned his head and looked at me, grinning. 'Go back to sleep.' he laughed. 'There's nothing on the road. You're imagining things.'

The distant figure slowly, very slowly, raised an arm. A hand for a moment fluttered, waved, and then settled into an emphatic stop signal.

'Stop! Stop!' I yelled again. 'Please – you're going to run it down!'

The driver continued to chuckle, and my friend muttered, 'I can't see anything.'

Suddenly, the young man beside me yawned and stretched. 'Wha . . .

What's going on?' He sat up and looked through the windscreen. 'Good God, mate!' He grabbed at the driver's shoulder. 'Pete, slow down! I see something on the road. There's definitely a figure there. Right there. Look.' He pointed. 'Oh God, it's waving. It's waving. Stop. Stop!'

The figure now suddenly loomed closer. Both hands waved in desperate appeal. I heard my friend gasp as she saw it for the first time. She screamed.

The male voice beside me yelled, 'You're going to hit it! It's right there! You're going to run it down!'

Peter's body suddenly stiffened. A shocked, anguished cry burst from his lips as his white-knuckled grasp on the steering wheel tightened. 'I see it. Yes, I see it. Now I see it too. Aaagh!'

His foot hit the brake pedal, and the small car bucketed and slewed from side to side. The road angled unexpectedly into a sharp left-hand curve. I realized the pile of broken timber I had glimpsed as we careered past was probably the warning sign for the sharp bend ahead.

Peter held the shuddering steering wheel as he forced the car into a frantic direction change. The little car made the corner in a sliding, slewing, body-jarring movement that shook it savagely. The windows rattled alarmingly, and the contents of the glovebox fell out and sprayed across the floor.

We slithered to a violent and abrupt stop. The massive trunk of a fallen tree totally dominated our view through the windscreen. The car had come to rest in the thick foliage and branches of an enormous ghost gum. The tree's fall completely blocked the road only a metre from the bend. Its leaves swallowed up the small car. Had we not stopped, the impact with this tree would have killed us instantly.

We struggled to get out. We pushed at the doors, breaking off twigs and leaves. In snapping, crunching urgency, we forced our way through the debris to the corner. We didn't speak. We couldn't. We were all in shock. We were also too frightened of what we might find on the road.

We reached the corner and stood shivering, huddled together. The road was deserted. A soft breeze gently caressed the red soil. It sent spiralling eddies back along the way we had travelled. The moon shone brightly on the trunks of sentinel white gum trees, and somewhere, a bird called. It was peaceful and incredibly beautiful.

Like an ache, the beauty impacted us forcefully. *We were alive.* We knew it could so easily have been otherwise. We were the only ones there. There was *no one else.* In the profound silence, we stood motionless, instinctively tightly holding hands. It was a long, long time before anyone could move.

Who? What? Questions about the figure remain an unanswered mystery. Only to the people concerned does the memory evoke a poignant reality. Four grateful young people survived into comfortable old age.

Through the years, I have flashes of vivid memory. In startling clarity. I see again this lonely red country road. This strange figure with desperately waving arms always has frantic appeal. but the spiralling vapour covers it all with gentleness.

Tragedy was averted that day. I do not know if the others remember as I do. I do know I never took my life for granted again. Even the police recorded surprise that a carload of young people had *not* been killed.

Amazing and undeserved grace is my heart's response today.

CHAPTER 6

Growing!

T he spiritual lessons I had to learn came to me clearly and a bit frighteningly when I went away on holidays as an adult.

The first coach holiday was a three-week safari into inland Australia. I travelled about twelve thousand kilometres and saw much of the heart of my country. The journaling and the inspiration became the basis for my novel *Beyond the Ashes.* What I personally learned spiritually educated me further along my quest to find the *right* way for my life.

We stayed overnight at Ayres Rock (in more recent times, this rock has returned to its original Aboriginal name of Uluru). This is a stunning place in Oz, and the changing colours as the sun sets on the rock are difficult to adequately describe. The spectacle takes your breath away.

I walked around that rock in darkness, after dinner, on our last night camping there. I remember to this day impressions of looming evil spirits, although I carried a torch. On the other side of the light beam, *swirling* disembodied shapes followed wherever we walked. The other people walking that night were joking and happy, yet in my spirit, I *knew* something tragic would happen in that place.

When the tragedy of the missing baby occurred only a few years later, I knew only *the truth* – greater than the sensational story of swirling lies, hype, coverups, etc. – would one day be revealed. The fact that the baby's parents were Christian made what they had to suffer understandable when I always sensed forces of evil were also warring against any truth about a dingo the mother was trying to voice.

I acknowledge from that time that I believed in the existence of *evil* in the affairs of mankind. I also came to believe that humans can be possessed or taken over by that *evil* if they choose to look for it or relish playing around in dark areas of life. 'Hidden' evil becomes powerful when humanity seeks after it with deliberate intent.

My second encounter with this reality of unseen forces came a couple of years later when I stood at the tip of Cape Reinga on the North Island of New Zealand. Standing on that windswept point, I listened, as our Maori guide had told us. They believed it was from there that the souls of dead islanders left on their journey to eternity. My companions stood reverently with heads bowed.

I too stood head bowed. Suddenly, I was aware that I could sense the presence of spirit entities. Not all were leaving. Where were they going? Had some gone in one direction? Where indeed would others spend eternity? It was not peaceful for me in that place. There was a sighing on the wind. I felt deeply disturbed.

I met a Maori Christian before I left New Zealand, and he significantly helped me on my own journey of discovery. He told me for generations, tribal islanders in the Pacific had been told it was *light* that would lead their souls to eternity. When they heard teaching from Christian missionaries that Jesus Christ *is* the Light *of the world*, it helped thousands find their way to the salvation message of the cross and accept *Him* as Saviour.

He taught me a prayer: Matua-O-Terangi A-Men. In essence, it means, 'May Almighty God bless you, more than I can imagine or ask, out of His storehouse of blessings.' Matua-O-Terangi A-Men.

I realize today this was a significant shaft of *gold* in my life.

CHAPTER 7

Navigating the 1960s — Learning and Growing, Turmoil and Discovery

Societal Explosions

The turbulent 1960s brought in a 'spiritual' dramatic shift to our whole world, few realized, at the time the impact. For the young, it became an exciting smorgasbord of *choices*. Climbing, ambitious role models of the same age as the emerging adults brought the focus onto music. This was proudly shouted by onstage charismatic youths.

With this gradually came a lifestyle change to 'free love' communes, the beautiful images of 'love-ins', and flowers and beauty, music and 'freedom'. It was even proclaimed on the new transistor radios (gifts of love to young folk and seniors), who now heard, '*It is the dawning of the age of Aquarius.*'

Indeed, teenage culture began to drive by deed and actions this new proud way forward. Most, at the time, did not – and many still don't –*see* it for a 'counterfeit' culture. All things of the occult became normal, while 'drugs' and 'feeling good' – *whatever makes me happy* – appeared by definition to be OK. Society was being led into a pit.

Many of the emerging adults during this period sadly fell into this morass. Many seniors in the 2020s still want multiple choices regarding morality and decision making – The adage written so long ago: *I am the Captain of my soul* (John Donne) still resonates with truth for them.

Leading mentors began to hunger for 'soul' food and proudly proclaimed they had found the answers. Through their music and appeal, they pointed to mountaintops and brought Eastern religion as a great flood into lives and yearning spirits. Many began to follow the Dalai Lama.

Yoga and other health practices – which, within themselves, were not dangerous – became a normal part of life. Deeper deceptions of the occult came in subtly. All forms of expressions in art, paintings, and extreme music and even lewd stage performances were gradually embraced.

People spoke to the dead under the guise of 'helping' humanity. Teacup reading and mysterious forms of fortune telling were marketed and often displayed as games for children. This was not a visually violent decade, but what began to be seen came by the emerging media influence. What appeared on stages and in cinemas would have been shunned by a society who, after the Second World War, longed for entertainment to be uplifting and beautiful.

The subtlety of the sixties as I lived through it was that it was *in* our lives, and the Christian Church began slowly to shift focus on how to be *relevant* and worried less about the message Christ died to proclaim.

Sadly, with rising technology, the message of the church as a united entity has become more fragmented. My personal journey is my tribute to our Mighty God, who, by His shafts of gold, kept me seeking for only *Him.*

My Journey through the Uneasy Sixties

Returning from New Zealand was a difficult transition. It was to have been a working holiday. I loved the lifestyle, made many friends, and settled into a pattern of more settled life, including a commitment to a small church family. Everything at home had changed. My father's heart scare meant plans for early retirement for my folks were now in place. Relocation of my home life would now be necessary.

I was offered my job back at the *Courier Mail.* I was delighted but knew after a couple of days, I could not return. I sensed my return would bring 'friction' as others had slotted well into my previous positions. No one said anything, but I *knew* my return had destabilised the office situation. I felt welcomed but unwanted.

I made a sad decision to go into another area of training and applied and obtained the position as secretarial office assistant for one of the leading gynaecological surgeons and specialists of his day. My two years with this brilliant and loved Catholic doctor educated and enriched my life in ways only fully understood many years later.

His passion for the sanctity of human life and his work with the hospital, staffed by many who were in sacred nursing orders, opened my mind into deeper spiritual areas. There were pregnant patients, women, and men, with their desperate longing for children, and the question of abortion was a resounding moral question in this workplace. The issue of preserving and guarding of *all* life was an absolute here.

Two women I remember particularly were battling medical opinions that told them there was *no* chance that both their children and their own lives could be saved. Unusual and difficult circumstances heralded the cry 'Abort! Abort!' The team accepted them as patients. They could offer no *certainty* but prayer and the best of medical care. Dr Cary and the wonderful Mater Hospital supported these courageous women, and *all* acknowledged with thanksgiving prayers that God gave them a 'miracle'. Both mothers and their babies survived.

'Only God! He used our hands and our medical expertise to bring about His will in these circumstances.'

Valuable spiritual lessons were learned by me during my brief time at this place. Looking back, I see this as a *shaft of gold* I have remembered and am grateful for my whole life.

Personal life now took centre stage, and things spiritual, I thought, took a back seat to *living* my life. Feelings of restlessness and loneliness emerged, and as a young woman, my desire for my own children was quite strong. However, stronger even than that was this inexplicably hunger, and the big questions hung in the atmosphere. *What is life all about? Is there a more important purpose for it all?*

The ease with which I could adapt to the spiritual forces of the societal sixties shocks me now, but at the time, it was an interesting journey. I found an affinity with the fortune tellers, card readers, and others of clairvoyant persuasion. I was fascinated with communicating with the dead, which an esteemed lady Doris Stokes brought to our attention when she toured Australian capital cities.

Scientologists conducted a series of fascinating lectures and training programmes down the street from where I worked. Enthusiastically, I began twice weekly night-time classes. I loved it! There was a mentally stimulating and beguiling aspect to it all. I began an examination which stretched my mental capacities supposedly for *higher illumination.*

I completed my assignment. *I heard a voice.* I understand and thank God now for this *shaft of gold.* I heard *clear* words.

'You will close your book. Leave it on your desk. Politely say good night and leave! You will never come back here again!'

It was so clear and emphatic, I didn't stop to think, 'Who spoke?' I left. I never returned.

When I told my dad, he was surprisingly understanding and said, 'Girly, find your own path to life, but stay in the *light*.'

I took up water skiing and ballroom dancing. Both were energetic and enjoyable but did not solve the issue of personal inner loneliness. People around took notice of the externals. I still worked hard to accomplish something visible. I was delighted the day I dropped one ski and became a slalom skier. Inside, I was still alone and felt 'lost'.

Two girlfriends, who are friends today, were part of the ski group. Both were Catholics and always went to *mass* before coming to ski. I admired their commitment and lifestyle.

One mentioned to me quietly one morning, 'I would be afraid if I did not go as it is my Sunday *duty to God.* It begins my day well, and I know I will be kept safe from all harm.'

This confidence was shattered a few weeks later when a dear friend of theirs was killed by an unlicensed driver as she walked home after attending mass. *What is life about?* The question rose again in my heart.

Outings and dates, for me, had always been enjoyable social occasions, and having been brought up in an age when clear moral guidelines, provided by parents, dictated 'no sex before marriage', I can remember only two that caused upset or concern.

One was an army soldier who, on the way home from our signals training during our time in the CMF, tried to hypnotize me. I pretended he had succeeded and listened as he suggested various ways we could have sex. Then he said we could begin immediately. I must have worried him as I passionately proclaimed it was my life mission to remain a virgin and any man who violated that would die.

I remained quietly pretending to be asleep as he went through his performance to 'wake me up'. We never spoke of this, but he always treated me with respect. I never knew if he really believed his hypnotism had worked.

John – my friend John had been a friend since primary school days. This was quite acceptable when we were children but subtly changed once we became teenagers. I had never thought of John as being dark skinned. I knew he was an Aborigine. His skin always seemed to me as a coffee colour – not that I ever thought too much about this. He was my friend and was, to me, a valued, polite, and caring companion.

I was innocent of racial differences because this aspect of life never had touched me personally. I went with John to see the opera *Macbeth* in Brisbane's Grand Majestic Theatre. It was a very societal occasion, my first experience of an opera. I loved the theatre and the drama. What happened in the foyer was not dramatic but painful in its hidden yet obvious display of disapproval. Matrons whispered behind their hands one to another, and men coughed, looking and sounding embarrassed. A few feet shuffled nervously.

John and I walked through the people back into the street and returned to his parked car.

He said to me with anger in his voice I had never heard before, 'Faye, I'm so sorry. This was not a good idea. It is because I'm black, you see, and you are very blonde. We have breached a hidden societal acceptable normal.'

We never went again on what would be viewed as a date but remained friends. He phoned me to say 'goodbye when he left Brisbane to complete university studies.

During the 1970s, he was featured in news items and became a leader in the formation of a tent embassy and as a keynote speaker for Aboriginal rights. He often looked frightening and militant in action and behaviour. I struggled to see in his face the gentle one I once knew.

Sadly, his personal life deteriorated. News and rumours spread that he had committed suicide. *What a terrible waste of a talented, educated, and beautiful life.*

Back in the 1960s, my spiritual questions were still about the possibility of a *God Almighty,* someone who would care for *all people*, a being beyond colour, race, or ability – *one* who cared for *all*. How could it be possible?

***

CHAPTER 8

Mid- to Late 1960s — A Journey of Rough Personal Seas and Heart-Challenging Events

What is this life about? Still to be learned.

A new male addition to our water ski group made an impact on us all. His impact on my personal life was *profound*. He is remembered as being important but not for the reasons at the time I thought.

George was fun! He was an accomplished dancer and water-skier. He was tall, spoke well, and appeared confident and capable. We became skiing and dancing partners. He told me he loved me, and I loved him. I was happily convinced he would be my life partner. *(Why was it obvious in later years that because he was not a Christian and his main life passion may have been for accomplishments and not for spiritual truth, as mine became, it would have been a disaster?)*

We became engaged. I had a pretty but simple engagement ring. We booked the church. My parents found, booked, and paid for the reception. My wedding dress was beautiful with a veil and long train. The few weeks ahead were lived with excited anticipation.

The invitations went out, and as George had no living family, his list was confined to work colleagues and his best friend, Kerry, who was his flatmate and appointed best man. Mine was close family and friends. My cousin Joy was to be my matron of honour.

Nine days before the wedding, I heard George's voice for the last time.

He said, 'I need to talk to you. Can you come down to the street café?'

I could not leave my workplace. A patient had begun an early labour. I simply could not leave her alone. I had to wait for the doctor to arrive. I explained simply that I could not leave her unattended. His sad-sounding response chilled me, but I was too busy at the time to fully comprehend.

He said, 'Perhaps this is the best way. Talking to you, you would persuade me everything could work out. But I know you deserve a better life. I must leave.'

He simply went! From that day to the present time, more than fifty-five years, he has never been seen. He simply *vanished*

*Th*ree letters were left.

1. He informed his boss that he was leaving. He never came back to collect owed wages.

2. Kerry was advised that he would not be returning to the flat and to make sure I knew his small car was parked down the hill from my place of work. His car and his water ski were for me. (I sold both and helped my folks cover venue cancellation charges.)

3. My shocked parents found a letter in their mailbox: 'I'm sorry . . . I must go. I have no other choice. I love your daughter. This is best for her.'

The church minister was also astonished. He could offer no insight. He confessed that he thought well 'of the young man'. He offered comfort and prayer and could not contain his composure when out of my mouth came a statement that *stuns* me when I remember.

I said, 'I don't really know much about God, but it seems to me that when a door slams shut so emphatically, one day He will open a window with a higher perspective.'

That kind man touched my shoulder and said, 'May it be so. You have more faith than you yet *know*. Bless you.'

I did not know where the words I had voiced came from. Inside, I felt shattered into a million pieces. I had no body to bury, no reason to hate, no sense or reason for anything. It was like a massive, beautiful bubble exploded and my life was in bits.

The police were not interested in finding answers because he had left letters. A private investigator found only that he had received a package from Somerset House (believed to be his birth certificate, needed for the wedding) the day before he left behind his whole life. Even the apartment George had been secretly working on as our future home and a surprise for me was, a few months later, bulldozed to build an overpass.

Nothing, it seemed, was to remain. I wondered if, inside, I would ever unfreeze. Love, sexuality, beauty – everything felt...*frozen*.

***

CHAPTER 9

The Beginning of Spiritual Clarifications

The Journey Continues

The following weeks were lived in a vacuum. I functioned but felt more directionless and lost than I would have believed possible. Work was difficult, and in my heart, I knew I had to leave. A constant stream of pregnant patients once inspired dedication and commitment. Now it was 'stressful', and each day I longed to escape.

Dr Cary encouraged me to sit for a public service shorthand and typing exam. I was pleased to learn I was selected to work in Canberra, Australia's growing capital city. Air fares would be paid, and hostel accommodation was available. I was to work as a private secretary. The information about which department and for whom I was to work was to be advised later. It was an opportunity for a new beginning, and I accepted with appreciation. There was no joy but a peace which surprised me.

At my interview, I told the public service appointments officer I would prefer to work in a small typing pool, if this were possible. He was surprised because of the high secretarial ratings I had apparently achieved. I felt to tell him my *real reason* for changing jobs, and he kindly agreed to my request. A couple of years later, I discovered my personal information was placed in my file. This was, I believe, why my working experiences in Canberra were such a joy.

My job was in the Department of Education and Science, and I worked with three other women on the eighth floor. We were the smallest typing pool in the department and were valued. All of our typing was on the highest quality of paper, and we typed letters mostly confidential in nature. Typing accuracy was expected to be 100 per cent. It was a great place to feel hidden and secure, and the three older women were wonderful supportive nurturers.

My wonderful parents in Queensland were concerned. They were now retired, at the Sunshine Coast. My hardworking dad enjoyed his fishing. My mum painted and played her piano accordion. They would have been delighted for me to live there also, but after a couple of weeks' holiday, I knew my decision to relocate was right.

I reassured them, and still, with this inexplicable frozen centre inside me, I left for Canberra. It was approaching the end of the 1960s, but the final months of this decade were to be, for me, a *huge learning experience* whose events prepared me for the 1970s and the beginning of what has become my *life*.

*****

CHAPTER 10

Canberra

Twists and Triggers

C anberra and hostel life were rich in social experiences, and life was *full.* There was little time for contemplation or wondering about the future. I merely lived life. My job was satisfying and productive, and I had somehow achieved a 'frozen inside' personality, and many friends and colleagues thought of me as the *icy blonde.*

In retrospect, I believe I held myself erect, did what I had to do efficiently, and probably emitted a strong 'Leave me alone!' straight-backed, untouchable aura. David told me years later he remembered my Isadora scarves and the way I tossed my head. They swirled around. It was apparently a bit intimidating.

I was involved in many social activities. I loved swimming, skating, and tenpin bowling. Amateur theatricals in Canberra were also a loved and welcome pastime. I made friends and joined clubs but never really 'connected emotionally'.

One dear friend I made at tenpin bowling was engaged to a man who was a driving instructor. So with her encouragement, driving lessons with him became part of the mix. This was the background to which the *trigger* incidents opened the future for me.

Valleys and Mountaintops

I was in Canberra when man landed on the moon in July 1969. *It was tremendously exciting.*

I went home for six weeks. My younger brother and his wife had lost their premature baby girl after only a few hours of life during this year.

This tragic event brought a compassionate response from the army processing officer for Vietnam War conscripts a few months later. This man told John to go home. He would not process the enlistment form. One sad event in their young lives had probably protected them from future heartache.

The Vietnam War was a tragic background to all our lives in the late 1960s and into the 1970s. Many lives in the generation a few years younger than me indeed suffered much. Many did not come home. Life and rapid changes all began in these years, and the pace has quickened ever since.

***

Returning to Canberra brought . . . *triggers* that were rapid and life defining in my personal life.

No. 1

I bought a raffle ticket. The money raised was going to a veterans support charity. I was not really interested in the prizes. *I won!* A huge crate of expensive wines, beers, and assorted liquors was delivered to my room.

Someone added my *room* number to the announcement of the winner on the hostel lounge notice board. It was not the management. I began to have night-time visitors knocking on my door and inviting me to parties or others shouting for me to give them a bottle. 'Share, sister, share!' became a cry whenever I appeared.

Even some friends hosted more frequent parties, inviting me with a clear expectation of my contribution. It was a time of hassle and unwanted attention. I felt alone and vulnerable. I decided to keep one bottle of red wine (I knew it was a special vineyard variety) and asked at the office if the crate could be removed from my room.

I arranged for a new raffle to be conducted. When this occurred, a notice was clearly placed informing everyone that my balcony room no longer held such a prize. Eventually, I lost my new status of the 'balcony chick with the booze'. Thank od for the resolution of an upsetting problem.

No. 2 — Spiritual Turmoil

I went to a séance in a friend's room and was asked to be a mentor and leader because I was a 'spiritual person'. I went thinking this would be a distraction and *fun* (a warning here for those who think venturing into dark places, i.e. even Halloween stuff advertised as *fun*). You may have experiences but certainly not *fun*. This dark area of life must remain in the dark. Therefore, Christ is *the light of the world*. Not really *knowing Him* and being innocent is no protection.

What happened remains still a blur. Others claimed *nothing* happened. Most went away unaffected. One of the boys had nightmares for a week but finally got over it and always said 'nothing happened'.

Something happened! (With new insight, I believe – no I *know* something entered my thinking after this experience of darkness.) From my perspective, I saw and experienced images and events and terrible awareness of the spirit world which have only been diluted by ongoing development of faith in the saviour.

Back then, I was left with the scary thought that perhaps I had a gift like my grandmother and was meant to use it in the capacity of maybe a witch or a clairvoyant. This was concerning and left me *internally troubled.*

No. 3 — Unexpected and Unwanted Emotional Attention

A young hostel dweller who worked in the Department of Defense started joining me for coffee in the canteen before work. He was an entertaining and bright young man, a couple of years my junior. He reminded me strongly of my 'little' brother. When he visited me and asked me if he could share personal problems in his job and family etc., as a big sister, I was happy to listen. A few times, we sat on the balcony. He talked, and I listened. I enjoyed his company and genuinely felt care for his well-being.

When he was promoted in his job, our relationship suddenly changed, and I was unprepared. He began to shower me with gifts. He ordered flowers from the florist and filled my whole room with bouquets. Boxes of chocolates started coming and lots of other treats. He was now working long hours, and when I saw him, I appealed for him to *stop*.

He then stated he *loved* me. I was the kindest person he had ever known, and he wanted to marry me. I was shocked! All I had ever shown was sisterly kindness. Now I did not want to hurt him but was scared that I had unintentionally given him the wrong signal.

I returned things to his mailbox at the front desk, but his gifts did not stop until he came one night and found me crying. I held a beautiful posy of roses. I was in the dining room.

'Please stop this!' I cried. 'I care for you but as a big sister and no more.'

He saw how upset I was and agreed that if I accepted one last gift and promised to never forget him in my life, he would stop swamping me with presents.

I agreed, and a few days later, a small package was delivered. Inside was a lovely pearl dress ring. For the rest of my life until it got absorbed among other items, I thought of John whenever I saw it and hoped life had treated him well. (I returned to Canberra for a visit and a conference many years later. I discovered he still worked in the defense department and was married with children.)

In the long-ago days, I was grieved by my own failures. It was distressing!

***

No. 4 — The Event That Almost Broke Me

Inside, confused, and a bit fragile, I concentrated on my driving lessons. I found the concentration and the open road soothing.

Two days before I was to take the driving test, the instructor gave me my final lesson – not just in driving but also in life, I realize now. He instructed me to drive off road down a lonely stretch of country road and to then stop at the boundary fence. I did exactly as he requested and stopped smoothly and proficiently.

He then surprised me by firmly saying, 'turn off the engine.'

It was then that my friend's fiancé changed radically. He moved across the seat and roughly grabbed me.

'How about it?' he growled. 'It's what you should be up for, and no one needs to ever know.'

'*No!*' I screamed in his face. I pummelled him furiously in his chest.

He moved away and vented his frustrations at me. 'You could have said no in a more refined manner. After all, it's what *all* you Sheilas really want.'

I was furious, not just with him but at the fact he had so little respect for my friend. I was sure with only two weeks before the wedding, Meg had no idea of his true opinion of women or loyalty to her.

I drove back to Canberra and parked in the hostel car park. Not another word was exchanged. I went inside and cancelled my driving test. I decided not to say a word to anyone, and some folks thought I had not been confident enough to go for my test. Meg looked a bit troubled when I told her I had decided not to take the driving test, but we both smiled as I did an impromptu 'chicken' dance to illustrate my reason for cancelling.

No one ever knew why, but that wedding did not go ahead. Although saddened, I was glad I had not told anyone of my experience. Besides, internally, I knew his actions evoked in me a feeling . . .

I wished I could have said, 'Ah, OK. Who cares?' The ice inside protected me. A strange, sad, depressed feeling of utter hopelessness now overwhelmed me. Was I somehow sending out messages into the atmosphere? Was something wrong with me? Was there a God? Did He care? Was I a witch? What about my dreams of one day being a writer? Why was I not writing anymore? Had something in me died?

Questions . . . questions . . . questions swirled. I went to bed and slept for hours.

***

When I finally surfaced, it was the next day in the late afternoon. I got up and showered and was eating cereal and drinking coffee when I heard my name called. Two of my dating friends, shortly to announce their engagement, stood at the door. Rick asked if I would like to go with them to see Lake Burley Griffin in moonlight.

'I would like to get a few photos,' he said.

Nola was enthusiastic. 'You will be amazed. It is *stunning!*'

I agreed to go. That night, I sat beside a stunning blue expanse of water washed over by silver/gold beams of moonlight.

***

CHAPTER 11

When Rick and Nola decided to walk around the lake, I was happy to remain by the water, looking at the beautiful scene. I sat alone on a lakeside seat. It was peaceful and incredibly quiet.

Suddenly, a thought came into my mind. It was like a gentle suggestion that fitted well with the breathtaking beauty around me. *Take your shoes off. The water will not be very cold. Think how far you could walk in and no one would see you. Imagine just letting cool, cool water wash over you. You could feel the cool water rising and washing away all your confusions and doubts. What a beautiful, beautiful night and what a peaceful walk.*

Trying to accurately record this now, it seems impossible that I could have had no other thoughts, not of family or what would happen if I simply kept on walking. (This, I now believe, in its beguiling and almost beautiful persuasion, was a result of the séance.)

It seemed *reasonable* and even *sensible*. I took off my shoes and walked straight into that beautiful lake on that beautiful night, and I just kept walking forward, one relaxed and steady step at a time. The soothing water rose higher, and I *knew* I would not stop. *Soon, it will all be gone – all the doubts, fears, broken dreams, and uncertainties of life. I will hurt no one else.* There was no thought of death; only the cool rising hope of *forgetfulness* was in my mind. The moon hung like a silver orb, and moonlight flooded the water's surface in front of me. The water crept up my chin and edged towards my nose.

Unexpectedly, the silent night was shattered by a booming sound. Was it in my heart? In my head? My ears? I can never explain. The words were clear. *Get out! Get out now! Your life is* not *your own! Get out!*

I stopped. Shocked, frightened, I turned around and surged back to the shore. Water parted before me in cresting, rippling waves.

***

I make no claim that God spoke loudly to me that Canberra night, but I can affirm that *all* I ever thought about who or whether He existed changed dramatically.

I walked back to the seat. I was dripping wet. I told my friends I had fallen in.

They laughed, and Rick smiled. 'I think you went for a swim.'

When I insisted on walking the two miles back to the hostel, only Nola looked at me intently. I smiled and waved. I watched them drive away. Then I burst into sobbing tears.

The walk home is lost in my memory somewhere, but I must have walked assuredly and with passion and determination. My clothes were dry when I prepared for my shower. I remember that hot shower as a kind of 'healing'. I remember the prayer I prayed later. I know I fell to my knees and asked for forgiveness. I asked for guidance as to how I could move forward and follow *Him*.

That night, I had a dream I went to university and studied languages. (This amused me because I had not been to university and always hated learning other languages at high school.) The next morning in the *Canberra Times*, the morning paper, I saw an ad: 'Canberra University is offering Italian language evening studies for adults. First semester – enroll *now!*'

Do it! This internal nudge prompted me, and the next week found me seated in a classroom. I had taken French at school, but this rapid Italian-speaking lecturer was fascinating to watch. She was able to speak more slowly in English, and her ability to speak a sentence at a time while we followed in our handbooks was helpful. I began to think one day I could maybe travel to Italy and search out my Italian roots.

The man beside me, who said his name was James (not his real name recorded here), seemed to find the language stimulating. I heard him exclaim, 'Amazing!' He appeared to be enjoying himself.

We greeted each other when we sat down to classes, but one night he asked me where I worked. We discovered we worked for the same government department but on different floors.

I thought no more about our conversation until a couple of days later, I was asked to deliver a tray of finished typed documents to the -fifth floor reception desk. I saw James sitting in one of the offices there and waved to him as I passed. He smiled and waved back. At Italian class, when he quite casually mentioned he was driving to see the early snow on Saturday and asked if I would like to go, I immediately said yes.

It is difficult to explain here, but somehow I *knew* there was not a man/woman friendship forming but a bond of companionship and of the mind. A deeper joining of the soul and spirit was to occur. I believe God brought him to me and me to him so *He* could reach us both, on our own life journeys, destined to be vastly different.

***

Driving back to Canberra after seeing the early snow, we stopped and got out of the car. There was a waterfall and a viewing platform about a metre from the road. It was only a small waterfall, but I was captivated by the fall of water and the sunlight filtering through the trees, which flashed and glinted on the white movements as it splashed into the pool below.

'How beautiful!' I exclaimed.

'How wonderful indeed are God's gifts to us,' James replied.

I nodded. His lips, for a moment, gently brushed my cheeks; it was as chaste and as soft as the touch of a butterfly. I looked up at him. I saw tears in his eyes and watched them slide down his cheeks.

'Oh God!' he cried. 'My whole life is such a mess!' He looked at me. 'Faye, can we talk? Will you listen to my heart? Please – will you not judge me? I am an ordained priest in the Catholic Church. I was sent here to Canberra for six months to "sort myself out". I need friendship and understanding. I'm sorry to drop this on you. I am in a mess.'

For the briefest of seconds, my heart dropped. *What next?* I remember replying, 'I'm in a mess too. Perhaps God has a plan to sort us *both* out.'

'I did not know you were a woman of faith, but I value your qualities of kindness and compassion. Some folks lately have yelled at me. Let's go for a coffee and talk then. Please come with me to the tiny Catholic church I saw down the road.'

I explained I was not a Catholic.

'Well,' he responded with a watery smile, 'I'm sure my God won't mind, and the priest will never have to know you were accompanied by a priest. Thank God He alone knows us by our hearts.'

I ha no idea where we were – somewhere south of Canberra.

That Saturday afternoon, I had coffee with James, and we shared in depth much of our hidden lives. He was only a couple of years older than I was but had scholastic achievements that were impressive for his age. He shared his faith and the dynamic story of a relationship with Jesus Christ that was beyond what anyone had told me before. My comprehension of Christian faith was expanded. I listened. I shared a little of my inside *frozen* feelings. He listened.

He prayed. I prayed. We prayed together. We went to church. I sat in that tiny church beside a priest, and we accepted with bowed heads and hearts broken bread and a sip of wine from a chalice. Together, we affirmed our acknowledgement of Christ's death on our behalf. It was probably different for him than it was for me, but I do believe God was there. I sensed a *holy presence.*

We returned to Canberra certain of friendship. We also had this hopeful feeling that God was going to restore us *both.* James shared with me the full story of passionately believing *God c*alled *him* to the ordained priesthood when he was 19.

'It was a clear path to me. Celibacy was and still is not a problem. I believe,' he told me, 'sex is a God gift, and I made a choice to consecrate this gift back to *Him* as an assurance of full heart allegiance to His call on my life.

'In the past year, a different problem emerged. I immediately sought understanding and compassion. I was a father now to many children in a children's home. I was called Father by many people. What suddenly became a problem was a deep, deep sadness because I would never have a child of my own. No little person would ever call me Daddy.

'There was a shift too with regards to women. I have never been troubled by viewing women as sex objects, but I began to now look at them through their potential as dedicated mothers of nurture and kindness. I never saw them regarding myself but thanked *God* for some fortunate man and children in the future. This was personal, and I felt my thoughts were not carnal. However, I longed to tell someone and hopefully ask God to never let my thoughts stray from my high calling. I decided to share with the bishop.'

James told me some of the horrible judgemental reactions he received from his church. He told me the bishop was kind, but others who were confided in were not.

'A nun who worked with me on a language program for orphaned children looked at me in absolute distain and said, "Father, you are a disgrace to your high and holy calling. All fleeting thoughts like that are carnally sinful." Another colleague, also a nun, told me I was *despicable*.'

I remember even now, when James looked at me (I don't remember his face), I saw a young man (only 30) with a light of holiness on his face but reflecting a human heart, both innocent and broken.

He asked, 'Do you think I am a despicable person and unfit to be a priest?'

'*No, I do not!* But I am *not* a Catholic. A vow of celibacy, even consecrated and deemed sacred – if it stops someone from expressing normal human feelings or asking for help, I feel something is *not* right.'

I believed I was 'unsuitable' to be a competent advisor for him but thank God He was certainly with us both 'as friends'. James said on one occasion that the archbishop had given him 'six months to sort himself out'. The Department of Education and Science had given him a meaningful job, hoping he would work it all out in six months.

'I know only God can sort me out. I will always think of you with gratitude. You have listened and are listening without judgement and separating the man from the priest.'

I nodded. I knew only God could sort me out too. James helped me to find the straight path to knowing *who* God in Christ really is. His years of training enabled him to listen and understand. He was not fazed by my recounting of gifts that had accompanied my journey that I knew were of God but were *supernatural* in nature.

He advised, 'Know God loves you. He will light your path but only if you follow light and never again satisfy curiosity about dark ways.'

Neither of us had any knowledge of Who God the Holy Spirit really is, back then. It was going to be many years before I learnt about God the Holy Spirit and *who* He is in His vital role in the trinitarian nature of God. I pray today that if James is still alive, he also has expanded his vast bible knowledge, surrendered to the cross, and been baptized in God the Holy Spirit.

The future for us both was still ahead in January 1970, but the few weeks we had of occasional cups of coffee, in-depth talks and 'listening', and praying prepared us both for God's purposes. One hurdle still, without prior notice, confronted me. The department head who had recommended me for my job called me into his office. He looked incredibly angry.

'Please, Faye,' he said kindly. 'Will you be seated? It has been reported to me, in strictest confidence, that you and that James man on the fifth floor have become good friends. Is this correct?'

I nodded.

'Has he told you he is a well-respected ordained priest from the Sydney diocese? He came here on a work basis. His appointment was a special contract.'

'Yes,' I replied firmly. 'He told me. We attend Italian classes. He is a good friend. You have no cause for concern. Our friendship is based on unique experiences and is one of listening and caring companionship. He helps me, and I hope I am helping him.'

He nodded. He did not understand and simply said, 'Be careful, dear. You are the last person who should be taken advantage of by a "rogue" man of the cloth.'

'James is *not* a rogue,' I responded. 'He is a fine godly man of impeccable character!'

He looked at me. He sensed I was annoyed. He was fiercely protective but trusted that I was telling the truth. He closed the matter, and actions perhaps planned were averted. Thank God!

Only a couple of weeks later, James phoned me at the Gowrie office. It was after dinner, and I was surprised.

'Faye, God has spoken, and I am returning to Sydney tomorrow. I will deal with my own lacks as He is opening for me new doors of opportunity to help broken and needy people. This *call* on my life is higher than any personal feelings. I will see the archbishop in the afternoon. I am hopeful of His approval and full restoration.

'Thank you. You may never understand what your friendship and understanding has meant, and probably, I may never be able to tell anyone about the kind blonde girl who was the God key to my restoration. Thank you and may He guide and lead you onwards to know Him more and more. Bye and God bless!'

'Bye, James, and thank you.'

Godly wisdom and guidance was his gift to me, and as I held the silent phone in my hand, I offered up a prayer that indeed God would honour his decision to return to his consecrated life. As a non-Catholic, I was uncertain but incredibly appreciative of his human sacrifice to his Godly calling. For me personally, I sensed a new beginning. I thanked God for my friendship with James and knew in my heart his help with spiritual tangles would enable me to focus forward.

***

CHAPTER 12

1970 — Lifechanging, New Beginnings (In Retrospect, Wow!)

17 October 1970. A new *journey*. Fifty years
celebrated on Hamilton Island, October 2020.

***

I n early 1970, I continued Italian classes. I concentrated on work and still enjoyed the small private working environment of this typing pool (as it was classified). We were responsible for typing, sometimes multiple copies on ministerial executive letterhead, highly classified documents.

I was also involved with a supporting role in *The Caucasian Chalk Circle*, a stage production based on the Bertolt Brecht adaptation of the Bible account of King Solomon and the two women and their fight over one child. I enjoyed my small (perhaps three minutes on stage alone) part where I had to portray an hysterical village woman whose own child had been kidnapped.

I threw my full passion and heart into this role, and when the play was selected to go to a drama festival in Wagga in New South Wales, I enjoyed travelling there also. This Wagga event occurred later in this extraordinary year. I was driven by my then fiancé, David, and met some of his Australian family connections. I wonder today if, because their first glimpse of me was on that Wagga stage, they thought of me later as a very *volatile and passionate* person.

There is much to the story of this incredible year, but events moved rapidly.

End of January 1970

It began when I decided to cancel my place on a coach hired to travel to Sydney to see the stage production of *Hair*. Everyone was excited, and I knew many were also disappointed when they missed out. I really did not care about going. I cheerfully surrendered both my theatre ticket and coach ticket. Now I looked forward to a restful time at home.

On Saturday morning, I slept late and strolled down to enjoy a hostel breakfast. The room was eerily empty, but David was already seated at the end of our usual table. I sat at the other end. Silently, we ate our breakfast. It was a strange feeling, this long table and us, perched like birds, at either end.

After a time of silent eating, David looked up and said, 'Faye, would you like to go for a picnic beside the river?'

I had no idea what river he meant but intuitively *knew* there was probably nothing I would rather do than go for a picnic. I think I said, 'Yes, I would indeed.'

Neither of us was seeking a long-term commitment, but that simple afternoon picnic on the bank of the Murrumbidgee River began some enjoyable times together. We went to the ballet. We saw an opera. We dined out and visited coffee shops. We went for long hikes and swam and picnicked beside the river on several occasions during the closing days of summer.

Time flew, and gradually, both of us had the unconscious awareness that 'being together' had become important. I was uncertain if I was emotionally ready, but *God* had gone before.

***

David came to visit one night in July and said, 'I love you. Will you marry me? If you do not love me, I will not be staying in Canberra.'

In a blinding *flash*, I knew I could not imagine life without him. Wherever he wanted to go, I wanted to go too.

I said, 'I love you too, but I am a bit scared.' (I'm not sure what of – but I think a lingering fear of being hurt.)

We walked to Proud's Jewellery Store on Main Street. On a chilly Friday Canberra evening, a commitment to each other was begun by the purchase of a beautiful diamond engagement ring. (We both loved the single stone with two golden hearts forming the setting clasp.)

The next morning at breakfast, we stunned everyone who knew us and who had not realized we were dating by our happy announcement: 'We have set our wedding date for 17 October and have booked All Saints' Church, Ainslie, just down the road, for a morning eleven o'clock service.'

We planned to be married quietly without fuss. David's folks were in England, and since my dad's heart attack, my own folks were not travelling far from home. The church rector said he would happily marry us even if it was only him, David, and myself, and two witnesses.

What was planned in the next few weeks takes my breath away even now when I think of it. The women I worked with excitedly planned a garden party–like wedding breakfast, tables and chairs in one of their beautiful gardens, and they, with financial support from my family, cooked the meal.

It was expansive and varied. We had a beautiful wedding cake, which one of them also made. Lavender wisterias bloomed in September, in Canberra, and the garden setting surrounded by wisteria was expected to be photographically perfect – if only it did not rain.

When I understood that a totally private wedding was not going to eventuate, I made certain we visited my family in Queensland, told near and far friends, and we invited friends in Canberra to be the bridesmaid and the best man. One of my work friends' husbands volunteered to accompany me down the aisle as a stand-in to 'give me' to David as a father figure. I remember Theo with gratitude for his strong support on this exciting day.

I went to speak with the gentle, godly man Reverend Chynoweth, who was to marry us. Two weeks before the wedding, I was anxious and a bit worried. I told him of my concerns that I would not be able to love David the way he deserved to be loved. I told him I still felt a bit frozen inside.

He laughed. 'You two will have a good marriage. David came to see me yesterday and said the same thing. He told me he was worried that he would be unable to love you the way you deserved to be loved because of his very reserved nature. My dear, you are approaching this day with the right heart attitude. It will be my great honour to perform this service. I'm looking forward to it.' He added, 'So many come to this point in their lives, and their most important question seems to be "What's in it for *me*?"'

The month before, when we were returning to Canberra after a few days in Caloundra with my folks (probably in mid-August) (I remember it was a bit *chilly*), we stopped at a beach named Urunga on the New South Wales north coast. We loved its private wildness and beautiful expanse of sand. David booked a 'special' room at the guest house, and the owner was delighted we had chosen it for our planned two-week honeymoon.

Walking home to my hostel room after my talk with Reverend Chynoweth, I began *now* to have great joy and expectancy about the wedding day and the beach holiday to follow. No bride could have been happier or more confident of the future. I thank God for that gracious, godly man, and I am grateful that years later, we named our property in a rural area 'Chynoweth'. We will always remember his kindness and gracious help to us both. Chynoweth means, in Welsh, 'new home'. It remembers that man of God's Welsh ancestry. He later became a bishop and was well loved in all parishes he oversaw. We were saddened to learn of his death sometime in the 1990s.

I managed to contact Father James in Sydney a few days before the wedding, and he sounded pleased. He said he would say a special mass on the day and remember us in his prayers through the years. He spoilt it a bit by adding at the end, 'I will not forget you, Faye, and, in my heart, hoped you would become a Catholic. You would have made a *wonderful nun!*'

I told David, and I know he was *not* pleased. I knew I wanted to truly serve God in my life and still believed I could know Him more and, even as a wife and mother, be a productive Christian. Spirituality issues would be dealt with in God's perfect timing.

Saturday, 17 October 1970

Intermittent rain showers became a normal pattern during the first days of October. All the spring disturbances arrived. There were strong wind gusts, storm threats, and overcast and dreary days.

On the night of the sixteenth, I prayed. 'Father [I was really only beginning to understand our relationship, but I did not think He'd mind if I asked Him] please, will You bless the new day to come?' I asked Him to let it be a day of beauty and peace. I know I asked for it to be sunny but also added (as I believed it in my heart), 'Rain or shine, if David is there and it is our wedding day, we will give You thanks and rejoice in it. We will be grateful for Your grace in bringing us together no matter what the weather.'

***

I had moved from the balcony room in the hostel to a ground-floor temporary room. David was already living in our rented, recently built apartment in a new suburb called Fisher. We would return there after our honeymoon.

On our wedding day morning, I woke up incredibly early. I parted the curtains. The dawn sky was ablaze with colour. It was a dazzlingly beautiful early morning with the promise of a day of bright sunshine. My heart soared. *I certainly could not go back to sleep!*

The bridesmaid and best man had already left for the church when Theo arrived to pick me up. I was dressed and waiting. My lacy wedding dress and large picture that would cause many comments in future years. In 1970, Theo accepted my mini dress and large hat as being beautiful and appropriate for a morning wedding.

He said, 'Lovely!' and folks in the foyer clapped as we walked out to the car.

The service was memorable. The music was beautiful. It was a more elaborate service than I was expecting. I remember it as being triumphant, deeply spiritual but meaningful in every way. I had not asked about an organ as I was only focused on us and our commitment to each other. The church, the minister, and the organist who played with passion and faith – the whole service was like a royal occasion.

Several people came unexpectedly from the Department of Education and Science, and our quiet morning service for *just us* became a remembered occasion for many. Mr. Mitchell, a departmental head, told me later it was the most meaningful and beautiful wedding service he had ever attended.

A Shaft of Gold in Remembrance

I know God was with us (we did not know it in reality then). We accepted it more as an abstract kind of blessing and were thankful. The garden party was lovely. There were tables and chairs across the lawn, and purple wisterias tumbled profusely over walls and in garden trellises. There was food and drink in abundance, and the air resonated with laughter and fun.

When it was time to leave for our long drive north, we found our car had been gift-wrapped with reams of toilet paper, and tin cans were strung out on the road behind us. Laughing, we managed to fight our way inside the vehicle after removing many of the tin cans. We did not, however, even notice the smell of rotten fish until we were some miles along the highway. That rotten fish became an unwelcome gift left at a Sydney service station. A helpful young man finally found the wrapped putrid object firmly wedged under the car's chassis (we had creative friends in those days). He was highly amused, and we left Sydney with shouts and whoops of well wishes resonating behind us.

At Urunga, a beautifully laid table greeted us. There were flowers and a bottle of champagne in a bucket. A card read,

Congratulations, Mr. and Mrs. Roots!

17 October 1970

The first morning of our new life together, we breakfasted on the lawn.

Then we began our two-week holiday. We had days of sunshine, and like two small kids, we revelled in beach walking, exploring the small coastal community, and picnics behind the sand dunes. We ate numerous rum balls – one of the Canberra lads had given us a massive tin of them to bring with us.

We spent wonderful days of glorious freedom – swimming, relaxing, laughing, and enjoying being together. No one was there to worry about us, so we could come and go, eat and go to bed, and wake up as we desired. We knew we had made the right decision by coming here. We could dine out or bring something in any time day or night.

In 1970, Urunga was an unspoilt paradise. I'm sure in 2021, it would be a bustling place like all Australian coastal townships are now. Progress and prosperity! I am glad of these honeymoon memories – two weeks of an almost *Robinson Crusoe*–type of existence.

CHAPTER 13

New Life Together

We returned to Canberra on the last day of October 1970, to our apartment in Fisher. It was brand new, only recently completed. Friends had gift-wrapped chairs, tables, and available objects with toilet paper. The rooms were all decorated, and even when we returned to work the following week, loose strips of paper were still being discovered in corners and under chairs and table legs. We laughed and still remember the joy and fun of our remaining days in Canberra and the wonderful friends we had there.

David was selected for a teaching position at the Brisbane Anglican School for Boys ('Churchie'). He was surprised, and we were both saddened by our imminent departure but pleased by a new adventure in Queensland. He was to begin at the end of January 1971 for the first term.

Our first Christmas as a married couple was spent bush camping on the banks of the Murrumbidgee River. We had a bush tent, an open fire in the sand, and an improvised table on a cardboard box.

Christmas Eve

In the beauty and peace of this star-studded night, I was ashamed to find that the nostalgia for the glitter, music, shared carols, and family around former Christmases suddenly hit me, and warm tears slid down my cheeks. David's encircled arm comforted me, and we knew that onwards together, we would make our own new memories. The peace and startling beauty of this night with the gentle murmur of the river held a quality of inexpressible beauty and hope. It was wrapped in a clear remembrance of what Christmas Eve really celebrated.

We began to sing 'O Holy Night' and 'Unto Us a Child Is Born'. I do not have a good voice, but David's clear tenor voice soared. What a beautiful Christmas Eve – memory for a lifetime and above a canopy of black 'star-studded' glory! How blessed we felt!

***

Christmas Day

I awoke to a beautiful surprise. David had decorated a small fir tree with streamers and bells, and seated beside the fire, we breakfasted on kippers and toast. No fancy cookware but fireside toast and kippers boiled in a billy stays forever as a taste of remembered enjoyment.

Turkey pieces and chicken sealed in bags served with a small salad and followed by Christmas cake, rumballs, and fruit was our lunch, but ahead of us was a wonderful afternoon of walking, sleeping, swimming, and enjoying the isolation and joy of being together. This was only my first real certainty of God's presence with us, but I look up to heaven now and thank Him for the memory.

***

CHAPTER 14

The 1970s

1971–1980

A bit sad but excited, we left Canberra and arrived in Brisbane a week before the commencement of School Term 1. We were fortunate in being able to rent a house overlooking the Brisbane River with a cross- river service accessible after a short walk along the path beside the property.

The house was close to David's working environment, and I could walk to local shops or cross the river by ferry to the city. What a wonderful location – appreciated now in fullness so many years later. How different the entire city is today, and riverfront houses, even old ones like we rented, would be worth millions of dollars. This city life offered much to us. We had live theatre, opera, ballet, music recitals, and ease of access to cinemas and leisure parks. It was a great three years which passed quickly.

I obtained a position with the Drake Employment Agency and had many interesting and varied positions. One I was scared about was with a law firm. I was not a trained legal secretary, but the new partner was keen for me to come for his first month with the company. A secretary was part of his contract, and he explained that he really had no work for me as he had worked long hours to get it done before he came. He asked me to be gracious and polite to his clients and partners and to pretend to be busy and always occupied. I remember this as one of the fun times of being a temp secretary. I typed happily most of the day. I wrote much in the line of my own stories and rekindled once more my passion to be a storyteller. I completed a section of my later book, *Beyond the Ashes.*

I was part of morning tea get-togethers and happily tidied up and looked after things. At the end of the time there, he gave me a glowing reference, and this impressed the Drake Employment people very much. I was worried about getting another legal position, but my next employer asked me to stay permanently. They were a clothing manufacturing company. Their offices were just across the river from where we lived. I travelled to work happily – until I became pregnant about a year later. I was sick, whether it was morning or evening – the rolling of that little ferry, pleasant before, became a nightmare.

David had only stayed the first term at the prestigious boys college, and I too felt relief when he left. My social encounters with other masters' wives had left me with a feeling of 'not quite fitting in with the social order of things'. David worked for a short time in a clerical capacity at the Myers Emporium but was delighted to be given the chance to work in primary teaching. His first posting was to Wynnum Central Primary. Folks were still there who remembered little blonde Faye. What joy that he was still there when our first child was born! For one very elderly lady teacher, this was an exciting event.

The years 1971–1980 were years of significant life changes. Now in Queensland, we saw my folks at Caloundra and met up with other family members on picnics or at the beach. One of my favourite pictures of David was taken at Caloundra with our baby on an early visit to Nana and Pop.

Proud Dad, 1972

During this decade, we were blessed with three children – our daughter in '72 and sons in '74 and at the end of '77. We bought a house and land in one of Brisbane's outer suburbs, and life was busy and fulfilled.

Where was God? This aspect of life would soon emerge. Every child was a wanted family addition, and we thanked Him for the shafts of gold each one represented in our life – each one a unique and special child. I remember feeling exceptionally blessed.

Below is a photo on Caloundra Beach in January '78.

Arms of *Love*

While living at Ellengrove – the outer-Brisbane, almost rural suburb in the 1970s – I read an article in the local paper. Not a lot of people in this report supported the idea of a small church being built in the nearby emerging new suburb. I am not sure why, but I wrote a letter in response. I know it was inspired.

One comment I made – 'There is "death is the heart" of any community where God is not honoured' – seemed to touch the developers, and a small church became part of the plan. An Anglican clergyman appreciated my letter and began to visit occasionally. On one of his unplanned visits, I learnt a valuable lesson.

My two beautifully dressed older children were left for a few minutes while I returned up the flight of stairs to collect the baby. We were all then going to catch the bus for a shopping outing to town and a fun day in the park. I found my laughing children excitedly jumping and playing in a small mud puddle caused by overnight rain. They had even made a couple of mud pies. They were mud-splattered and dishevelled. I heard the bus coming. Despair flooded my soul. I sat on the back steps and cried.

Reverend Graham arrived unexpectedly. He looked at the scene and said gently, 'Faye, come and sit with us.' He took off his shoes and socks, rolled up his trousers, and sat down **in** the mud puddle beside the two little ones. 'These children were sent by God for you to enjoy their childhood. It will pass in the blinking of an eye. Seasons will come, and seasons will go, and what really matters in the end is *love*.'

I sat with that man of God and the children beside that mud puddle and know today it was a *shaft of gold*. I longed to know the God he told me about as we talked, a God who loved him and he loved with all of his soul, mind, and body.

***

CHAPTER 15

At the end of 1978, David was transferred to a country school. These transfers were a necessary part of a teacher's life. David was told this transfer, if accepted – because of family status – would probably ensure him a few years of stability with no surprises of a far outback posting while our children were at school.

Imbil in the Mary Valley shares the heritage of Gympie, the main centre's rich colonial gold mining past. For six and a half years, this town was our home. *We loved it!* We lived in the large Queenslander schoolhouse right next to the school. The house itself was surrounded by a massive paddock where horses often roamed free. After a frisky stallion snatched the stroller with Kevin inside and ran away, challenging me to chase after it, only young animals were later contained there. The local policeman who witnessed the event rescued my incredibly happy youngest child who had enjoyed the game. I remember I was completely *shaken.* An enjoyable memory was being able to watch the children walking across the paddock as they came home from school. David settled into teaching, and Alison was in Grade 2. Colin attended the new preschool.

As a family, we began attending the small Anglican church (Christ Church). Although it began as a 'good thing' to do, being the new teacher and his family in town, it became something extremely important. It was as if God met us there. This church, this community, and the Christian faith which *ignited* there changed our lives forever.

Many Christians were at the school. Several staff members, including the principal and a few families, also attended Christ Church. A strong family bond developed among the school community and the local town. Reverend Lex, his wife Rhonda, and their family became dear friends of ours. We highly valued Lex's shepherd calling and his passionate teaching on the Person of God, the Holy Spirit.

In the early eighties, there was a wave of spiritual renewal which swept the world. Imbil was no exception. Going to church became a joy, and a love for Jesus as our Saviour and Lord enriched the lives of all. Even in Gympie City, talk was heard about the revival taking place in our small place. Lex came to our house one weekend and asked if he could pray and lay hands on us so we would be baptized or filled with the Holy Spirit. We knew by his teaching that this was a certainty of the *fullness* of the Trinitarian Godhead in our lives and that the *truth* of the Word and who Christ was and *is* would be revealed to us.

We had no miraculous occurrence instantly, but both David and I *know* life for us changed forever. We did not see instant manifestations of His presence, *but* we can see now we were 'born again' into His kingdom. We know fifty years later, we are still being changed. Through all our failures and mistakes, He is still working *in* us, and it began so long ago.

For me, teaching about God the *Spirit* helped clarify that He gives holy gifts to fulfill His purposes. His way is in *light*. The counterfeiter who cannot create disguises with deception his gifts, which mimic the divine but come to fruition in *dark places*. The intention is to water down God's plan for the salvation of *all* of humankind's souls.

For me, because of my sensitivity to the unseen realm, I had to learn to *trust* His gifts and pray for the revelation of any circumstance where I needed clarification to determine His will. This became the worry in later years because I often sought clarification from trusted folk within the Christian Church who were so worried about rocking their comfortable boat, they did not have a helpful answer. There were many times when folks were of the opinion that either I was a bit loopy or that I had eaten something that triggered a vision, dream, or revelation.

Bless all the dear ones as my life unfolded who did not *know* or have an answer but who prayed with me and *for* me.

There was a lot of family pressure in the early Imbil years. Childhood illnesses became rive in the school, and our older children caught both measles and chicken pox, one after the other in a cycle. They recovered quickly, but it was a stressful and tiring time. David and I also had bouts of normal winter illnesses.

Our youngest became ill dramatically and unexpectedly. He was hit by measles and chicken pox together as a double whammy. To make it worse, he also developed a glandular fever side effect. When he was admitted to hospital, the doctor prepared us for the worst.

'It is unlikely he will survive the night,' he said.

David and I prayed. That night on the veranda of that old home, I spoke with God in the deepest sense of communication I have ever known. I began by a desperate acknowledgement. *Lord God, you gave us this fine son. I know he is your child too. I'm asking You to heal his body and return him home to us.* Anguished and sobbing, I remember the strange unplanned addition I made to the prayer. *Lord God, if it is in Your will to take him back to Yourself, I'm asking, Lord, that You will give to David and me Your strength and Your courage to face the days ahead. In Jesus's name, Amen.*

I lay on the bed beside Dave, and our grief was raw, painful, and real. We surrendered him into God's hands. After a time, peace replaced our anguish. We went to sleep.

***

I woke up suddenly. It was black, like the middle of the night. My senses were instantly aware. I heard a swooshing sound, and the black night seemed to be sucked out of the room as if by a vacuum cleaner. Soft velvety darkness gently floated back into the room. All the crystal items on our dressing table began to glow with vibrant orange lights, and the silence was profound.

I felt myself rising off the bed. I looked down, but I was still beside David. I looked up and felt I could touch the ceiling.

Then I heard a voice. It was powerful. I was peaceful and not afraid. I heard clear words. *Your son will not die! He will come home tomorrow. He was born with a purpose to fulfill. It is a kingdom purpose! Do not be afraid!* The room returned to normal as I sensed myself being gently placed back in bed.

The next morning, I drove to the hospital and was greeted by excited staff. I was told of a 'miraculous' breaking of a high fever and dramatic recovery. Kevin greeted me with an excited cry of *'Mummy!*

The sister handed him to me and said, 'Take him home.'

I left immediately and enjoyed a singing, laughing journey home.

The phone was ringing, and the annoyed doctor informed me he had not given permission for him to leave.

'He should have stayed for further tests. Bring him back.'

I think I shocked him when I explained my truth. 'When I was told to leave, I left. God told me he was coming home today.'

No one argued with me.

In the church later, Reverend Lex said the vision I had described had appeared in a documented account of 'visions and God' in a book on the *supernatural.* He held Kevin and prayed for us before we happily returned home.

For a few weeks, life settled down, but after another series of illness woes affected us all, I began to feel devoid of energy, exhausted and depressed. I could not explain, but my doctor was wise and helpful.

'There is no pill which can help you. I'll have a word with David. My prescription is *go away by yourself for a few days.* You are spiritually and mentally *exhausted.*'

I hated giving David a heavier load in his busy life, but friends from the school and church offered help. Somehow, I *knew* these couple of days, like a retreat, were, for me, a *God gift!*

CHAPTER 16

A Beach Encounter

On that lonely beach called Castaways during the brief time away, I had a moment when I sensed a holy presence. It was very real. I dropped to my knees as the merging of clouds, sea, and sky enveloped me in warmth. I felt *undone*. I wept. I prayed for a clean, pure heart and asked to be available to Him in whatever way He would lead.

That night, I wrote my first inspirational prose that was an answer to my young daughter's question.

She had asked me, 'Where do you see God if He is invisible?'

This was the answer I wrote down on that long-ago night. This began my writing journey, first with simple poetry proses and then later in more prophetic, revelatory, and historical fiction with a Christian heartbeat.

Where Do I See My God?

I see my God in the early morning when hills
are tinged with gold.
Almost indescribable beauty of a brand-new day unfolds.
Green fields, green trees,
Grass wet with morning dew,
The fresh, clean smell of a summer morn
And warmth that flows right
through.

I see my God in the faces of children at silent prayer,
In the radiance of their trusting, childlike faith.
His presence is positioned there.
I see Him in the miracle of a newborn child at his mother's breast.
Joy and wonder in her eyes communicates to all.
Everyone around is blessed.
In a grief-torn house, faces ravaged by sorrow and care
Suddenly find His peace and strength.
Divine love has found them . . . right there.

In love, compassion, and kindness.
When people care for the sorrow and trials of others,
My God is always *there.*
He shines from the eyes of a brother who feels for the needs of his friend.
Where people genuinely love one another,
His Blessings never end.
I see my God in the struggle of a little bush rose to bloom;
Choking weeds and nettles have barely given it room.
It struggles against impossible odds for its face to reach the sun.
When it succeeds, its sheer beauty
Radiates glory to everyone.
I've sometimes felt like that myself, searching to find my God.
More prickles and setbacks than sunshine,
But my longing for Him lives on . . .

I pray, Lord, that when I reach my goal,
the face that is turned upwards to Him
Will be like that little bush rose,
Alight with inner joy *to make other folks think.*
Where is my God?
He's out there in the Spirit within the reach of all.
In every facet of human living, He is within everyone's call.

Christ came that we might accept and follow.
What a better place this world would be
If each person would realize their need and take a minute to pray.
O Lord, my life is an empty void; forgive me.
Please send Your Spirit to fill it.
In the name of Jesus Christ, saviour of human souls
And Lord God Almighty!
A-men.

***

The writing of the first prose began a different kind of spiritual journey. Many times, I expressed in these gentle written expressions of life with Christ a reality I was only myself fully understanding. Many folks expressed appreciation for this prose, and I enjoyed making books and illustrating them with pictures.

Rhonda and Lex Carey took me to my first Aglow meeting in Nambour in 1979. In those early years in *Australia*, it was a worldwide women's ministry. Men of God from different Christian denominations became advisors. This first Aglow meeting gave me the longed-for fulfilment of what I had hungered for from childhood. In that meeting room, we came together as God's people, loving Him and not bothered about the signs on our own church doors.

A husband and wife ministered. He was a Catholic, and she still worshipped in a Presbyterian church. Together, they led the worship to Christ, and the girl who accompanied them on the piano was dressed in a Salvation Army uniform. The vision for Aglow was birthed deep into my mind at that long-ago meeting.

Lex told me as we travelled home that he was an advisor to the newly ratified Aglow gathering in Gympie. I went to my first Aglow meeting in

Gympie in 1980. Spiritual life for me was changed, secured, and challenged. I learnt more in Aglow than my own denomination was then teaching. Jesus Christ and His lordship was firmly established in my faith life. (During this time, I suffered sorrow and rejection from dear Christian friends who did not believe that in this wave of spiritual renewal, we were not being deviated from *the way.*)

In Aglow, teaching on gifts of the Holy Spirit brought many of us into the understanding of Pentecost and *all* the gifts. In Aglow, the gift of tongues was explained and accepted as part of being 'born again' into the Spirit. (My traditional church was not accepting particularly after Lex and Rhonda were called by God to minister in a North Queensland mining community.)

The years ahead had many challenges as I lived as a mother, wife, and woman growing in the things of the Spirit but faithful in every way I was able in my own place. Thank God for David, that in understanding and growth, we were side by side. He supported my Aglow commitments through the years.

He was supportive when some of the supernatural gifts that I had known from childhood began to appear. What *joy* but what responsibility was now mine as I understood so clearly as a more mature Christian what a clever counterfeiter Satan can be!

Thank God *He is* the Creator, and how real and evident this must be in the discernment of the gifts of His Holy Spirit!

***

CHAPTER 17

1980-2000

These were twenty years of incredible growth in understanding of God, His gifts, His callings. I studied at Bible college by correspondence, and creative writing became a passion, a joy, and brought pain. I wrote about my Saviour but also wrote as He led and inspired books about life and real people. I wrote fiction, historical with fictional humans in the story, but I suffered with them as their journeys unfolded. I wrote stories about teddy bears with children in mind, but the stories always had a heart of God. These bears remain in a collection of forty, and each teddy has his own story. All these things began to unfold in the years ahead, but the two decades in this chapter are a view only of the beginning of understanding of God, His creativity, and His giftings. *Awesome God!*

I wanted to be knowledgeable of the craft of writing, so I also took a creative writing course by correspondence and graduated during these two decades. I have two certificates: Vision Bible College and Australian School of Writing (both probably unknown today, but I learned *much*). My greatest teacher in the things of God was and is God *the Holy Spirit.*

***

The decade of the 1980s is a remembered time of great swirling of life. The children were growing up rapidly. There were commitments to our church family, ensuring our older folk were visited and kept a part of our lives. David's mum and dad visited in 1976, and for a few years, our older two children were convinced they had grandparents who lived in an aeroplane.

All of our lives were enriched when these loved seniors from England emigrated and came to live in Gympie. This was a special time for us *all*. The children now had two granddads and two grandmothers. There were rich memories of beach visits and celebration gatherings at both residences in Gympie and at the coast (something both David and I never had growing up, both my granddads died before I was born).

Sadly, my dad died at the end of 1980, Dave's mum in 1995. Both Dave's dad and my mum lived to see the turn of the new century.

***

Our new life on a property began when we purchased thirty-three and a half acres of unimproved bushland in 1980. We paid no more than we would have paid for a small house block closer to town.

I remember how opposed I was to consider buying this land. 'It's too remote. What about the children and their education, health issues, snakes, etc.?'

I was passionate. I knew this would be *wrong*. David suggested we pray and decide the following day. I will never forget the clear answer I heard from God in the night. It was the exact *opposite* to what I wanted or thought was *sensible*.

When I woke up the next morning, my heart-wrenching worry was that someone else would buy it first. I love this land – its trees, its native inhabitants, even the snakes/spiders and other creepy crawlies, each of which must be kept to its own territory.

This property we purchased and named 'Chynoweth' has become for us – even in our latter years – a source of sanctuary, learning, and peace. This name, remembering the church rector who married us, is Welsh for 'new dwelling place'. We had memorable times and enjoyed family camping here until we were able to have a house built.

We moved to live permanently in January 1984. It was sad to leave Imbil, but we retain special memories of our time there.

For our children, a new local school meant travelling four kilometres on a bus. There were new challenges and learning for us *all* – no power or running water, a generator, a gas stove, and a gas refrigerator, tank water (learning to be careful with water usage), and discipline to get homework and other chores done before the diesel generator was turned off (usually about 10:00 p.m.).

David, for a short time, continued travelling to and from the Imbil school. It was a long daily commute. He was transferred to a Gympie primary school. This school had a policy of staff total school involvement with no community commitments. David was, at that time, involved with the scouting association and with church responsibilities. When he was offered a teaching job at the new Christian Academy – an extension of the Christian Outreach Centre – he chose to go there and left the education department. He was appointed the first principal of this new Gympie school. It was a new life in the private school teaching profession. This school, in its beginnings, had a different syllabus and learning program for students.

Children from many Christian families not worshipping in the church attended the academy in the beginning. We, as a family, did not worship there; our own children chose to remain in the local schools where they were settled. It was a great but brief season at the academy. I worked as an aide and felt part of the life. Spiritually, I shared David's awareness that we were family, but the school and the church became intrinsically entwined denominationally, and we began to feel somehow like . . . 'aliens'.

When David left, he was unable to return to the Education Department. We had a lean and difficult period when his work prospects became limited. Any teaching appointments which became available had to be offered to young graduate teachers first, and there was a glut of graduates that year! David now found himself at a life crossroads.

Spiritually, both of us, however, continued to grow. We continued fellowship ties with the Anglican church in Gympie and later found a spiritual home in the small rural St Luke's Church in Kin Kin. The Gympie Aglow Fellowship thrived. I flowed happily and would have remained on a table of books and was called a publications chairwoman *forever* but, after eight years, knew God told me 'something' else.

I loved the spiritual growth in all of our lives in Aglow. We experienced wonderful growth as our Australian leader, Reverend Joan Morton, encouraged us as women of God to esteem our womanhood and our femininity. We learned valuable lessons about our Biblical identity as ordained by God and how to live for Him.

Amazing speakers came to speak at local meetings and international ones at conferences we were encouraged to attend. Seeing the world and fellowshipping with others outside our own 'comfort zones' changed us *all*. Thinking back, I am amazed at where I travelled with Aglow and how God miraculously made the way possible in more times than I can express.

I was on the committee of Gympie Aglow from 1981 to my present life in 2021, but it was not until 1992 that I clearly heard *Him* say to me that I was to *stand* as president – 'You are not to be *hidden* but to be recognized as a steadfast nurturer and leader in this place.'

Thank God for all the wonderful women and men advisors who have been on committees and supported through the years. Many, many have gone *home* – some of these my dearest friends. I thank God now for all the wonderful women and men who have been a part of us here in this small corner as we stood for *unity* in the Body of Christ and for Christ's message of salvation to the entire world.

CHAPTER 18

China, 1999

S elected to be part of a mercy mission organised by the China Inland Missions Organisation, the two small Aglow teams were part of larger missionary endeavours. I knew God spoke to me – *'Will you go where I lead you?'*

David told me on our way home from church that he believed God had challenged him to be prepared to release me to go somewhere he may personally not be happy about. At that time, Aglow Australia was ministering in far-east Russia and now to assist in China. Joan was leading a team to Russia at about the same time. Reverend Joan was responsible for the prayerful selection of the two small teams to China. One team was an intercessory team to widely travel and pray in various areas. The second was the mercy component. This team had a specific focussed goal.

When Joan phoned, she said, 'When I knew you were *called*, it was hard for me. Many Queenslanders felt certain they were to go to China. I had to make sure Australia wide, I chose *only* the ones God wanted. I prayed over all the names of leaders and others who had indicated missionary hearts on the table. I know your name kept leaping out. I know you are *called*. I pray you have heard clearly.'

Certainty flooded my soul. I had told only David about this feeling of *calling*. Now the focus of my life became China. I was scared, 'ignited', and prayerful. The Gympie Aglow family around me, including our valued advisor, were supportive in *every* way. I thank God in remembrance of 'strong mountain boots', a white hat with a huge sunflower, and a glove puppet resembling a duck with a movable mouth (word circulated about us visiting children) given to me with love.

Financial assistance came with donations to the Aglow Head Office, and this was forwarded to the missions as contribution for the provision of bottled water for all Aglow folk. We left Australia confident of care for our personal issues. I shared about the journey at both schools where I had RE classes. Teachers and children offered to pray.

One little fellow raced after me, a bit tearful. 'Mrs. R, I'm not sure God even exists, but I'm gunna ask "out there" for you to come safely back.'

I remember I hugged him.

The voice of the teacher went with me as I departed. 'We'll remember Mrs. R at the beginning of each day's lessons. We will do it and learn *together*.'

The story of the 1999 journey to inland China is full of complexity. I can only write what occurred and affected me personally. The whole world has changed much since then, but this was my reality and a brief part of the life I have lived. I knew God had *called* me, and because of *Him* and not my training or ability, events unplanned occurred.

In Hong Kong, swirling, grim-faced soldiers in red uniforms monitored our luggage and us as we moved to board our small plane to inland China. One of our ladies was escorted away to a 'detention room'. She was released quickly.

Our Chinese American interpreter Paul later explained. 'When she walked in with her grey hair and bright smile, one of the soldiers began to laugh. The sight of her happily claiming her confiscated bag with the thin letter opener, she had forgotten, seemed to reassure them she was not a "terrorist". "She's as old as my grandmother and could not even hold a weapon. I can't imagine her stabbing people," one young soldier had stated.'

We laughed but were reminded that caution and loving acceptance was our only way to journey.

Travelling remains now as memories of tortuous mountain roads, twisty and dangerous. I remember prayers often led in unison by Aglow women, which kept us God focussed, bus drivers with grim, unfriendly demeanours whose expressions changed as we travelled many places together. I remember seeing people working on high, dangerous-looking mountainsides (including little ones with small spades). I remember the child in a nappy who came out to greet the bus when we stopped. He showed me a large potato.

The interpreter translated. 'He said, "I am so happy today. I have found something to eat."'

We were accommodated in one of the most beautiful hotels I have ever seen; even the taps looked like gold. We were treated with respect and kindness by staff and all hotel officials. Our mission to help children was valued if we 'obeyed the rules'. Swirling red-coated soldiers were not to be our concern.

The Alley

We searched widely and finally located the nine children being cared for by elderly peasant farmers. It was in a remote inland town, and these children became our total 'focus'. There were abandoned girls, some with minor infirmities, and four boys with degrees of deformities or disabilities.

On the team, we had one doctor, two nurses, one speech therapist, a child-care person from International Red Cross, our Chinese/American interpreter Paul, and team leader Nita from Singapore. I was impressed by how perfect our Aglow unity as representatives of Christ melded and flowed on this team. We acted and prayed together as *one*. My main role was to interact with the children, 'keep them happy'. This was an absolute *joy*. My funny hat and glove puppet worked like magic as I clowned around.

Then in a moment, change came! One of the little boys with a walking stick decided to run as fast as he could down the alley, calling in excited Chinese as he ran.

'He wants you to chase him and try to catch him. Faye, be careful!' Paul called as I ran after the boy as he ran straight out into the street.

I tried to grab him as I exited the alley but was unprepared as a crowd of curious people surrounded me.

'I'm here!' I heard Paul shout. 'I have Timmy!'

I stood frozen. I had never experienced being engulfed by so many people in a crowd like this. Then, a wave of *peace* flooded me. It was like a shaft of anointing gold. I looked across a vast sea of Chinese faces, and a *love* for them all overwhelmed me. I held up the puppet, still on my left hand, and made his mouth open and shut. The sunflower bobbed up and down as I moved slowly towards each upturned face.

'I love you!' I said. 'I love you! And you and you.' Then I pointed towards the sky and said, 'He loves me.' I pointed to myself and then to them – 'I love you!' and 'He loves you and you and you.'

I smiled and saw many others smiling back. Then in my funny hat with the duck puppet, opening and closing his mouth, I spoke again. This time, I knew it was God's gift of tongues. With my whole heart of love, I stood there and spoke to the people.

Paul, at the debriefing later, expressed surprise. 'No one told me you spoke Cantonese,' he said.

Apparently, I expressed God's *love* and forgiveness to them all in their native dialect. I remember talking and feeling this love for the people deeply and profoundly.

Suddenly, a motorbike roared into the crowd. A red-coated, grim-faced woman yelled something. The crowd visibly lost all joy from their faces. She revved the bike and turned to glare at me.

I stood to my full height and, without conscious thought, lifted the puppet and, with its mouth, pointed to the young woman. I pointed to the sky with my other hand, spoke again. 'He loves you.'

I do not know what she heard, but she laughed. The crowd relaxed. We had a short but precious time of deep connection which remains a treasured memory in my heart.

That night, as we gathered for prayer round the table, Nita asked if we would be happy to spend another day with the children in the alley. We all heartily agreed.

She turned to me. 'Faye, would you be able to spend a bit of time talking to the people outside like you did today?'

I happily nodded.

'Apparently, you made people happy, and we have been granted a second day.'

The next day, I met two young men who waited for me on the street. They both spoke English and were doctors from a hospital in a remote mountain village.

One said seriously, 'Your speaking to the people helped more than any pills we can prescribe. When you return home, remember us, and my hope is you will return again one day.'

I knew then as I know *now* I never will, but memories, like God, are eternal.

I remember with gratitude, because of Aglow training in the dignity of godly womanhood, that I tried to always have a small touch of beauty in my suitcase to wear. This trip, we had severe restrictions on what we could bring and had dressed suitably and for comfort. We washed and re-wore most of our clothes.

Unexpectedly, one evening, officials announced that the government wanted to host a banquet to thank us for coming. I knew we should try our best to dress appropriately. I had a small cylinder inside of which I had squashed a light gossamer pink skirt and a pair of flat ballet shoes.

I dressed as well as I could that night, and when the rather difficult but grand meal was over (Paul had been expert at causing the spinning table to move on if something odd was in front of me; it was considered an insult if you did not choose something from right in front of you, and Paul helped by letting pigeon's eyes, beaks, or entrails or other delicacies I might struggle with glide past), Paul told me later that one of the Communist Party leaders told him to thank me for honouring him with my beautiful dress for the meal. Thank you, Lord, for Aglow teaching. The inexpensive squashed skirt had shaken out and looked quite pretty in the light even if worn with a much-washed white top!

On our final night before our flight back to Hong Kong, Nita asked me to wait up for her. We had just completed our prayer time.

'I believe,' she said, 'I am to buy a small gift for you and David. God spoke to me in the night. You will not find its significance for many years, but one day you will.'

She returned with two tiny jade communion cups. For years, we were faithful and committed members of our local church. The reason for these cups was a mystery. *Now* we use them as part of our Sunday service in our own home. We remember with broken bread and wine what Christ has done for us through His sacrifice at Calvary and His presence with us through all the years of our life journeying.

Memories of China remain poignantly *real* in my heart, and I rejoice that we now have a Chinese daughter-in-law and two grandchildren. Our grandson David was born in China. (Currently, this family are not professing Christians, but we, David and I, pray this will be.) I pray God's Kingdom purposes for us all will be fulfilled, even if not in my lifetime. Amen.

CHAPTER 18

Continuing the Unfolding Events of This First Decade in the Twenty-first Century: World — Spiritual and Personal Life

2001

A Simple, Gentle Tribute to Honour the Memory of All the Innocent Lost on 9/11/2001

A beautiful, gentle morning in late July 2001 *changed* my Christian life *forever*. I had a *vision*. It covered *all* of the sky overhead as I was praying (it was an Aglow prayer morning). The heavens peeled back. I found myself in a forest of massive trees – magnificent, proud. Three bolts of lightning came out of the sky.

In horror, I watched as one bolt struck one proud, beautiful tree. A second bolt struck. In the distance, I heard a third bolt. Everything began to shake. The first tree crashed. It fell on top of the one next to it. One by one, every tree began to fall like dominoes. It was as if the impact spread way beyond the here but was across the entire forest (Earth).

There was grief, incredible devastation as everything was shaken and stripped away. People grieved. There was sorrow and disbelief everywhere. Widespread violence and absolute horror ensued – not just people but also structures and old edifices. It was as if ordinary life was being changed and destroyed. I cried, but eventually, the shaking and the horror were silenced.

I heard the voice of God. *Look! Look!*

In a clearing, I could see people. They were all praying. Only one face was clear. It was Jane Hansen's, an American Aglow leader, and her grief was raw. I knew in that moment something really visually earth impacting was going to happen on the earth. It was going to be in America because I saw Jane's face.

In the clearing where praying people prayed, the ground was bare, yet just bursting from beneath the soil were tiny little specks of green. It was if new shoots would come to replace or even make better what had been before. *Hope* swelled in my heart.

The *voice* said, 'All things will be *shaken off*… but my K*ingdom will come.*'

When the 9 September 2001 tragedy of the Twin Towers happened, it rolled on our TVs, and what I had seen in the vision became reality in the day's events. Three others praying with me on that graphic day of the vision – 28 August 2001 – although they were praying in different locations around our town, had experiences of God that have radically altered their lives. One felt the earth *shake. Another* heard the words 'How the mighty have and will fall'.

The other dear friend (she went home in 2006) heard, 'This is the beginning of the end of the comfortable world, and the Kingdom Age *approaches!*'

The years following 2001, we have seen nation after nation fall. Kingdoms, churches, denominations, people of influence, and attacks on God's people have been unprecedented. All I could ever do was pray as the Spirit led, but in my heart was the hope of again 'seeing' the *hope* as I had seen the horror of the destruction.

P.S. When the 'bees' gathered in Orlando at the Aglow International Conference (unsure now of the year), I met a man from Washington who was an intercessor, and God joined us during a time of prayer about the conference. It unfolded in our later sharing that on the exact same day I had the forest vision in Australia, he, on a beach in the United States, had the exact same vision. It changed his life like it did mine. He, like me, prayed we would *see* God's vision of future Kingdom hope in our lifetimes. (He, like me back then, knew there would be only one ride for the ridegroom Christ to return to collect – but *how*?). *One day it will happen.*

***

Unfolding World Events Early Twenty-first Century

2002 — Australia received their first 'wake up to terrorism' call. The Bali Night Club bombing occurred. There was much sorrow and crying. Suicide bombers let bombs off inside a popular club and in a car parked outside – 202 killed and 209 seriously injured. Many lives changed *forever.*

2003 — U.S.-led forces invaded Iraq. Many soldiers and civilians died. Suffering will last for many through the passing years, even into second and third decade of this twenty-first century. Saddam Hussein was tried and hanged in this year. There was so much grief and uncertainty in the world. The church, despite rising world carnage, still appeared to be going on 'doing' the same and continuing cycle of *churchiness.*

2004 — On Boxing Day, a massive tsunami appeared – more than *two hundred thousand* deaths. Most nations on Earth were affected in some way by this disaster. (*Ten years later, in 2014, a man from Indonesia said to a media* *journalist, 'One incredible thing about remembering this event. Once upon a time, we spent our lives fighting each other. For ten years, we have not fought each other but learnt to care and love.'*) The horror of this Boxing Day event – children beheaded by debris, babies swept away, despair and human misery.

***

It truly was graphic and horrific, but I learnt a powerful, life-impacting lesson. I was in church on the Sunday following the news of this dreadful event. Dave was mowing outside, and for a period, I was alone inside. I was in absolute despair.

I knelt at the altar and prayed. 'I can't equate this incredible sorrow and loss with the divine love of an almighty God. Where are *You*? Where were You for all these innocent people? Many were praying for deliverance yet were swept into the ocean.'

I was vulnerable but totally honest. What followed will remain *forever* as one of the most graphic, exhausting, and revelatory experiences of my Christian journey. (I am thankful it happened in church and grateful that David was there to drive me home.)

Boxing Tsunami Vision

I heard the words 'Follow *me*', and I found myself as if I had been transported into the heart of the tsunami wave. It was terrifying. I felt the mud on my skin, heard the roaring water. For a period, the horror of bodies, death, dying, and helplessness was with me, the bodies of dead and dismembered children and the reality of 'feeling' I was physically there – in the middle of the carnage.

'O God!' I cried. 'If You leave me here, I will surely die.'

I felt as if dying was inevitable. I knew my breathing was erratic and the fullness of the graphic experience was swamping. I dropped to the floor.

Look up! Look up!

I looked up, and the cross on the stained-glass window at the back of the church seemed to be 'vibrating'. It was as if it was *alive*. Streams of golden light were pouring through the window, and the back wall was changed by a golden hue. I clearly heard the following words:

Because I am. Because I am the Christ. All things are in and through Me. I am in the very fabric of the world. I am in the tsunami wave. I am in the volcano, fire, and destruction. Because I am Saviour and Lord. My Kingdom will come!

One day every tear will be wiped from every eye.

Because I am!

Because I am!

The whole church was filled with this golden light, and *peace*, like a great wave, swamped me.

I remember nothing more except I know I prayed, 'Lord, if I am to die now, I am truly content.'

David found me on the floor about an hour later. Obviously, no one else came in. I came home with him, but it was *two* days before I could even . . . in an extremely limited way, share with him what happened in that little country church that day.

My reality, my truth, what I carry with me through life – I often longed to share and encourage others, but even within my church family at that time, it was almost too holy to be shared or even understood. Like so much, it became a part of the fabric of prayer journaling – and my life.

***

2005 — London reeled from terrorist bombings. Suicide bombs were set off in their underground rail systems. Later atrocities would shock the world. Pedestrians run down deliberately on London Bridge, and on a main thoroughfare, a soldier was beheaded.

Like all things, there was temporary shock and horror and, very quickly (particularly among Christian believers), a slipping back to the secure, comfortable and churchiness focuses. For the dead and injured, life changed forever, and for some survivors, life struggles to truly find sprigs and shoots of hope and new life in their damaged lifestyles would lead them to God and drastic spiritual changes.

From America, so many high-school shootings and lots of violence in the streets began in this first decade. It would accelerate until 2020's worldwide evidence of protests turning into anarchy emerged. Little was voiced about eternity, but many became self-focussed, and societies worldwide began the first baby steps into the phenomen of 'my rights, my justice'. Also, caring for the planet – a Christian ethic – turned into violence and political anarchy.

2006, 2007, 2008

Spiritually, these were personally quiet years. I journaled little outside the recording of great blessings from Aglow conferences and God's presence in and through many of life's experiences.

The deaths of family and friends impacted our lives majorly, but through tears and heart-grieving, there was always the hope of Christ and eternal destiny. Constant news from Ethiopia, Somalia, and Nigeria indicated cauldron pots of 'unrest'. There was lots of prayerful journaling. Still, I was acutely aware of 'not fitting' the mould of my church family but faithfully served in whatever way God led.

CHAPTER 19

Life Unfolding

The 2000s Continue: Personal unfolding of Life,
Marriages, Births, Personal Health Issues

Overseas Trip — Forty Years Married

God's Presence In and Through It All

The miraculous! The heart-searing and great *joy!* Three grandchildren were born in this first decade of the twenty-first century – a grandson in 2003 and two granddaughters in 2004. There was happiness and joy for those remaining in the generation before us.

It was a new and heart-grabbing experience for David and myself. Being grandparents evoked a great surge of *love* in our hearts but also an acute reminder of our own mortality and the passage and racing of the years.

***

2009

A personal crisis shocked me in 2009. I began having trouble swallowing, and thoughts of throat cancer surfaced among the medical and those around me. I knew the presence of God through all the tests – some of which were unpleasant, involving the swallowing of gooey gunk and small cameras on tubes.

When the diagnosis was discovered, I was grateful and ecstatic. I had a pharyngeal throat pouch, and although rare, an operation was considered preferable to laser treatment because of my age and long-term benefits. I thanked God for the diagnosis and surrendered to Him and the surgical competence of his team. Two weeks in hospital and being fed through a tube in my nose was preferable to throat cancer.

I had only a temporary life glitch. I met others on this journey who were not as fortunate as myself. I personally, again, experienced a wonderful and life-impacting lesson about God. This event occurred immediately after the operation, and even now, the incident remains clear and graphic.

He Spoke Peace

'This has been an outstanding result.'

The throat surgeon's voice lingered in my mind as I settled down to sleep. I was back in my hospital bed after the operation.

A few minutes later, I knew something was wrong. My throat felt swollen, and a bleeding lump had formed on my neck. There was blood on my pillow. I pressed the emergency button.

Within moments, the room was filled with medical staff. I heard a *code blue* alert resonate around the room as emergency people arrived from every direction. I knew a mobile theatre bed and a ventilator were near the door as well.

A nursing sister with coffee-coloured skin and a beaming smile said, 'Hi, I'm Blossom!' She lay across my chest and compressed my neck. She held on with both hands.

Peace — this one word resonated around the room and brought significant change. Everyone sensed it, and a calm relaxation touched us *all.*

'Yea, though I walk through the valley of the shadow of death, I will fear no evil, for you, my God, are with me.'

The words of Psalms 23 were alive and real in my mind. With Blossom on top of me, we settled into some place of such calm. I fell asleep.

The surgeon who had been advised of the emergency, while at a family wedding, came hurtling into the room. He told me later it was like walking into a wall of peace and well-being. It overwhelmed him as well.

The problem was discovered – a tiny nick in a neck vein had enlarged and ruptured when my throat swelled. Thank god it was not an artery. Repair was not extensive. I recovered well and, although fed through a nasal tube, was mobile and began daily exercise around the hospital corridors. I met several other patients as I journeyed. I recovered well and went home recovered and restored. I thank God for His grace. I give thanks for the doctor and the wonderful medical team.

I heard later that news of what occurred on that dramatic night spread far and wide. No one had an explanation. **It must have been** *God!* Memories of that hospital and all the other patients – I can only be thankful and grateful for His *grace*, undeserved but *real.* Many people I met in that place have journeyed on, some into eternity. *Thank God for my life!*

***

2010 — Guernsey and London: The Journey Continues

2010 — Married Forty Years, Guernsey/London

A Holiday

This 2010 journey across the sea will forever be a *highlight* in my life. David had saved in a holiday account so, on our fortieth anniversary, he could show me the significant places of his childhood. Together, we would make cherished memories in a place he had never visited – Guernsey Island in the English Channel.

This island – with its unique French and English heritage and its history of pirates, plaques, invasions, and even occupation by the Germans in the Second World War – is an incredible and beautiful place. We talked and fellowshipped with many kind and wonderful people. The Christian faith resounded in Guernsey – *we have endured much for centuries, and Christ has ever been with us.*

It was an amazing month followed by two wonderful weeks in England. The history, the life, the monuments, the buildings – everything was new and wonderful to me, and we have stored pictures to keep all the memories *alive.* But! This golden shafts memoir is to be more about God and His teachings in my life. Two miracles of grace occurred in Guernsey.

***

Walking the cliffs of Guernsey is an exhilarating, often tiring experience. There are well-maintained paths, many seats, and surprises of beauty to view along the way. I did not expect to find a toilet facility of elegant splendour on the high cliffs of this rugged island coast. On our second day of rambling, walking excursion, I saw it and marvelled at its cleanliness and beauty. The floors and walls appeared to have been hewn from white marble. Inside, I later discovered the pedestal basins were also made of this same grey/white marble. It all looked exquisite.

I ran out the door like an excited child. 'Dave! Dave! They are the most beautiful toilets I have seen in my whole life.'

I shot out of the door, missed the small step, and catapulted face first onto the granite/marble slab at the entrance outside. I heard the *thud* as my body connected with the granite. I felt shuddering through my entire frame. My first thought was *I must have broken many bones.*

A strange supernatural moment occurred. I felt as if I was bouncing on a feather bed. It was as if underneath were His sheltering arms. *A penetrating peace beyond description enveloped me.* David was in shock. He had witnessed the fall and was frightened, at first, to touch me or to try to lift me up.

I rolled over. I looked up at him. 'I'm OK! I am not hurt, dear. Please help me to get up.'

Praise and thanks be to God for what was a *miracle!* As we later sat overlooking the sea, drinking tea and coffee, and eating Guernsey gache (a tasty type of damper/scone), we thanked Him with all our hearts for what we *knew* was divine grace (undeserved) outpoured.

***

The second incident was later heralded by others as a *miracle*. I only *know* I prayed. David and I enjoyed the freedom we found on Guernsey. We walked, rambled, and generally explored everything. One busy day we had travelled on buses, walked along sandy beaches, and took photos and knew gratitude for a fine English summer.

As I was preparing for bed, I discovered my engagement ring was missing. Where could it possibly have come loose? I felt 'bereft'. I prayed and trusted God knew my heart. *Lord, I'm asking You for a miracle – undeserved*

– that my engagement ring will be found and returned to me. I value it for its forty years of memories and am grieved by its loss. Please, Father, may it be found . . . but if this is not in Your will, help me through the sorrow of its loss so I will not spoil this delightful holiday we are sharing together. In Jesus's name. Amen.

The next day, we tried to find it! The hotel staff searched thoroughly. We retraced as much of our previous day's travels we could remember, and although we met many gracious, kind people, we found nothing.

Before returning to our accommodation, we walked to the Police Station in St Peter's Port, Guernsey's main centre. The intention was to report the loss. Sadly, I spoke with the young female police officer who asked me to describe the ring's settings. When I did, she looked very emotional – I thought she was going to cry. A brief time later, she came back accompanied by a male officer with a highly polished ring held between them on a small stand.

'Is this your ring?' the young man asked.

I tearfully nodded. 'This is a miracle – an absolute miracle!'

The two carefully and gently placed it back on my ring finger. It was a beautiful moment, like a shaft of gold from heaven. I know I cried, and so did the young woman. The two men looked on, but both of their faces were alight with the emotion of the moment.

The story of the ring is lovely and amazing. A young woman was walking her dog late in the evening on the deserted Como Bay Beach. The tide was rapidly coming in. She knew she would have to hurry. Her dog suddenly stopped and began barking furiously at something in the sand. The tide was lapping at his feet, and he seemed desperate to retrieve it before the water washed it away. Diane could see moonlight reflecting on the object near his front paw. She picked it up.

She later told the police, 'I held it in my hand and *knew* its loss must have been intensely felt by its owner. The high setting of a single stone and two small golden heart clasps showed me it was reasonably old. I felt it was urgent to hand it in at the police station as soon as possible in the unlikely possibility that someone would come to claim it.'

'She brought it before she travelled on to work,' the female officer added. 'We arranged to have it professionally cleaned and put safely away. When you walked in the door and simply asked to report the loss of your ring, my heart pounded. You actually came!'

Amazing grace, love, peace, beauty, and joy!

Diane was an Australian who had worked on Guernsey for two years. It was unusual for her to be walking so late at night. Moonlight on Cobo Beach, the girl and her dog, the ring rescued from the sea – these images remain with me as blessed memories.

In Cobo Bay, the sea wall is an indication of how high the English Channel flowing from the Atlantic Ocean can rise here.

I am *remembering with joy and thanksgiving* the miracle of the lost ring!

***

An important addition to the Guernsey story: it was high on the cliffs of Guernsey that I had the second graphic vision of an earthquake in Christchurch, New Zealand. I saw the destruction of Cathedral Square, and tragically, in 2011, during my time away during Queensland's tragic flood, I grieved with others as we witnessed, on a hotel TV, the playing out of this vision.

(Few I spoke with believed me about this vision. Even an NZ Christian minister reassured me it could *not* be Christchurch. Wellington was on the earthquake fault line. Why God showed me must be an impetus *always to stay close to Him and pray*.)

INTRODUCTION TO CHAPTER 20

Thank God. Thank you to *all* who understood His heart. The butterfly journey was incredibly vast. It was *all about* God and *not* about me. I have problems expressing it adequately. I believe the Lord is leading me to write background details and then share from my prayer journal a few personal stories.

My desire is to protect individuals and the identities of communities and towns. Many still have butterflies flying. I give thanks to all who supported – Almighty God, whose *love* knows no barriers, His presence, lead, and strength on the way.

Thank you to Kerry-Ellen Logan, Aglow International Australian leader, and her wonderful team who knew it was 'of God' and supported with prayer and assistance with travel, accommodation, and meal costs.

To the unknown ones who gathered and sent me butterflies and little gifts of encouragement, I thank you. Thank you to *all* who prayed.

To anyone reading this who mumbled at the time that I should have been *doing* something more *important* to aid the relief effort, I can honestly say now my memories of standing beside a few folks in the centre of the cleaning and heartache taught me then and now that the ones who received and *knew* the *divine love* of God expressed by 'butterflies' were strengthened *in the midst of it all.*

Because I was not aligned on the journey with any denomination, I moved freely and could let God lead me. I made certain in every community and town that I found Christians who were gathering or helping and made certain they knew what I was about. We fellowshipped and prayed together.

An elderly lady simply walking and supporting, eating, and caring for folks was welcomed. A Catholic father who was part of an aid supply delivery team told me when we met he would not dare to touch or advise regarding 'the Butterfly Ministry' in any way. *It is of God!* His assurance of prayers was valued.

I was invited to go with them into isolated properties and be the Butterfly Lady. It would have been great to go if it were possible, but he was happy when I gave him a bag of small butterflies to dispense in aid parcels. His prayer of benediction travelled with me through future days: 'May butterflies fly into every needing heart. May they soar, bringing the promise of *hope*, *love*, *healing*, and *new life* wherever you travel. In Jesus's name. Amen.'

CHAPTER 20

2011

The Butterfly Journey Millions

The Australian monsoon season often brings a prolonged period of wet weather in mid-summer. In December 2010, a massive rain depression, driven by a cyclone north of the Queensland coast, triggered unprecedented rainfall over the entire state. Rainfall was so persistent and intense that for the first time in recorded history, every river overflowed and surged towards the sea. Tributaries could no longer flow into the main river and burst their banks. Water in a massive flood moved across the land. It swept into small towns, inundated pastoral lands, and swept livestock and crops away.

A dam burst, and one community in SE Queensland was washed away. Our news that night showed graphic images of cars with people in them, houses, fenceposts, and animals all being swept away. Three-quarters of the state was affected, and it was reported that at its peak, an area the size of Texas in the United States was waterlogged.

Long after the rain had ceased, the water continued to flow. This was heartache for many. As they were standing now in their drowned communities, longing to clean up, water still flowed over their feet. Our local community was built on the bank of the Mary River and frequently has floods. Gympie locals have a prepared evacuation technique to help low-level businesses.

In 2010, the crisis was not local in December/January but approaching slowly across the state in a wide ever-creeping tide. Local flooding would come our way, but the floodwaters from the north were, at this early start of the year, far away. My home is on a rocky ridge high above flat ground, and flooding is no problem. Exit roads and power failure can cause some difficulties if a monsoon is prolonged.

On 31 December and 1, 2, and 3 January 2011, the news and situation became worse. Small country towns were swamped, and residents of one were evacuated.

One report from a 92-year-old evacuated from a nursing home brought one lighter moment. As he was winched into the helicopter, he called out, '*Yippee!* My very first ride in a helicopter – and I'm very nearly dead!'

Other news of washed-away homes, missing animals, and vital infrastructure with scenes of heartache and grief were becoming more graphic. I journaled as prayers became sometimes as desperate sounding (I discovered on reading later) as the ancient psalms.

'O God!' I cried. 'What can I do? I am too old to help with heavy cleaning or lifting. I am too old to be of use, and I would not want to be "in the way", *but* in my heart . . . this desperate aching of grief. I know I pray and grieve for those who are grieving . . . yet this is *too much*. It is overwhelming! Please, dear Lord. Please do not tell me to just keep on praying. O God! O God! I sense Your pain as well. *All* who love *are* grieving. What can I do?'

The news on Monday, 3 January, showed that floodwaters had reached the town of Bundaberg – two hours north of us. A dear friend Gaylene now witnessed water everywhere in a town that had never flooded before. I phoned her, telling her my heart's desire was to stand with her and be of support and prayerful. That evening, she sent me a beautiful email card expressing the thought of how precious it was when people supported one another. The border of this card had *butterflies* around the edge.

On the morning of Tuesday, 4 January, I awoke in the early hours of the morning. It was still dark. The presence of God was overwhelmingly *real*. I went outside and sat down.

A voice said, '*Look up!*'

The Butterfly Vision

The sky opened, and I saw butterflies – all sizes and all colours pouring out as if from a heavenly fissue.

'There must be thousands!' I exclaimed aloud. A reply came. 'Millions! *Follow me!*'

I saw the butterflies were now on the ground. I could see them in the hands of children, people in the street, in schools, flying now over aid workers, ambulance helpers, Salvation Army workers, on boats, in buses. They were *everywhere*! Butterflies! Butterflies! *Everywhere!*

The words *new life, hope, peace,* and *healing grace* were in my mind. The vision faded. I returned prayerfully to bed and slept.

The first phone call came just after breakfast. It was my dear friend Elizabeth, and she asked, 'Faye, have you heard from God of some way we can do something in this dreadful situation?

I shared with her the vision of the butterflies, and I was astonished at her joyful reaction.

'I am so grateful and thankful. I heard God say to me in prayer as I asked Him what my daughter and I could do to help. "Ring Faye. She knows." How happy I am that I heard Him clearly and correctly! Butterflies and money will be posted to you today.'

I thank God for understanding and love from Kerry-Ellen and the team in the Aglow National Office in Perth. It was their backing and support that allowed this whole ongoing journey to commence. Thank God for my wonderful husband, who helped in every way possible by checking available trains, coaches, and accommodation possibilities. Thank God for His clear ongoing guidance as I felt I had 'stepped out of the boat' without really understanding precisely what or where this was to be undertaken.

Interstate phone calls started coming in. All I could ever suggest was finance to the national office and butterflies to me. I suggested the butterflies could be stickers or as elaborate and beautiful as they were available. Let us *all pray*.

I went to a small roadside craft shop and purchased the lady's entire butterfly stock. She expressed heartfelt gratitude and hope for the future.

'This has been a project for myself and our two daughters to earn a little extra to feed our animals. When the roads began flooding and the rain set in, no one visited. Our little business died. Now we can keep going with craft projects, and you have allowed us to hope for better days.'

I said, 'Amen' and silently prayed, *Thank You, Lord*.

Many folks in other areas bought their supplies from small craft shops, and it was as if God helped this way to stabilize lives.

I remember one gift arrived with an apology. 'Sorry – one of these beautiful blue butterflies is actually a dragonfly . . . Perhaps it will be appreciated by someone on the way.' (What a moment that dragonfly was to be in this unfolding story of God's miraculous grace!)

The roads north were still trafficable, as far as back roads were concerned.

David drove me north, and I spent three days with Gaylene and her husband. I little understand then what this would begin in my personal journey. Gaylene's community needed many weeks, even months of help and restoration. I had to return home because of advancing water and the beginning of road closures towards our town.

One incident happened before I left which pointed me clearly to the understanding that 'physical help and aid was how I could support', but spiritually, the butterflies were for 'inner comfort'. I saw a four-wheel drive parked beside the harbour as we were passing. It was a beautiful, expensive car. I had this 'inner' feeling I had to go over. I had no idea what I was to say or do.

She wound down the window.

Are you OK?' I asked.

She replied, 'No!' 'Can I help?'

'No one can. I wish I could die.'

To my surprise, she opened the door and hugged me as I sat beside her. She began crying, and I heard her story. She and her husband had built and worked for years to prepare a yacht for their dream six-month vacation in 2012.

'He died unexpectedly in June.' She sobbed. 'And then when the huge tide washed away boats from the marina, I saw the yacht smashed and then disappear out to sea on an enormous wave. I know I have people to care for me, but I have this longing now to simply be swept away as well.'

What could I say? What could I do? I was not trained in grief counselling.

I heard the voice of the Spirit say, 'Reach into your bag and take out a large butterfly and put it on the driver's steering wheel.'

I only remember now it was blue with silver sparkles on the edge of its wings. I heard her gasp.

'*Oh!* Thank you. Years ago, when I was a little girl, my dad told me, "A butterfly is God's gentle reminder that *He* cares. *He will carry you through.*"'

I continued to hold her; she continued crying, but the tears now were healing and not despair. She attached the butterfly to the centre of the steering wheel, and I remember sunlight shimmering on the wings. I believe in that moment, I clearly understood this butterfly journey had *nothing* to do with me and anything *I could do.* It was to be all about *Him.*

All the butterflies were stored in one suitcase, and I packed only the basics for my own needs. I carried a light hold-all bag with handles and went walking. I was an older lady simply visiting and 'connecting'. It became 'miraculous' when I never lacked what was needed and always had the *right* butterfly for the *right* occasion. *Only God!* I journeyed by train and on coaches wherever the towns affected could be reached. Even on the journeys, I met folk who had needs and wanted to talk.

'*Follow me,*' the voice of the Lord said.

I say now as I remember – that was *all* I could do, follow and 'listen to His voice'.

CHAPTER 21

Butterfly Stories

A Sample of Amazing Grace *Outpoured*

I travelled by train and coach however I could reach places. *All centres were happy to receive a visitor. This excerpt is from my prayer journal.* The overlander train journey took ten to eleven hours to get to the inland town and nine hours to get home (six hours was the normal estimate).

I returned home today, 27 May 2011, at [five] in the morning. The journey was longer than expected because many sections of the rail line are still suffering 'stress' from the enormous destruction experienced by the historic Qld flood this year. The teams of maintenance railway folk were a reminder that so vast was the destruction, sections of restored line need to be checked and stabilized daily. Sometimes we were barely moving.

Images remain in my memory, for out of the train window was a view of water destruction *everywhere*. Early explorers claimed they were looking for Australia's inland sea. So many died in the desert searching for it. Ancient legends had claimed there was an inland sea. In 2011, every outback town showed signs of being overwhelmed by water – a historic flood in *our* history.

At one railway siding, when the train was stopped by maintenance crews, one elderly railway man commented to all who would listen, 'We once had a huge wooden bullock on the roof of the pub. The water could not wash ol' Pete off, so it came in, with a mighty surge, and took off the whole bl——y roof. Pete was found in Ken Bristow's back paddock, still attached to the roof, fifty kilometres away.'

Coach journeys also became very, very long. With holdups, sleeping in strange places while waiting for connecting coach links was normal.

A Story Aligned with a Coach Journey

Our 6-year-old granddaughter expressed a desire to help poor people in the flood. She wanted to make butterflies. She used a *punch-out* tool to cut from thick cardboard thirty small butterfly shapes. She sprinkled them with glitter. I tucked them into the side pocket of my small handbag. I loved her efforts but had no idea how significantly they would be used.

It was the final journey to home. The expected time was seven hours and five hundred kilometres. It turned out to be an extremely difficult one. The coach was overcrowded, dirty, and hot, and the toilets overflowed. We were apologetically advised there would be *no* stops, and I managed to purchase one bottle of water and a muesli bar.

The journey dragged out, and after about five hours, I felt old, tired, hungry, and thirsty and longed for the rolling motion of the coach to cease. The constant delays because of landslides, road slippages, and crews still working to ensure safety on roads were jarring.

I complained to the Lord. *Father, you know how old I am. You know how tired I am. What about me?*

His reply shocked me. *Forget about yourself. Look behind you. Really* look *behind you.*

I turned around. In a flash, I understood that the coach was part of a rescue of displaced people stranded in outback places. The entire back section of this vehicle was packed with backpackers. Like sardines, they were crammed together – all young, all displaced, and all from other countries. While they were rescued as property owners desperately tried to get these young workers to safety, water kept rising, and they were kept on board, seeking sanctuary. Dirty, tired, incredibly sad, they were carried on and on. My heart ached.

I stood up, facing them in the jolting coach, and all I could say was 'I'm so sorry, guys, for this disruption to your lives.' Then without really thinking about it, I began to hand out the amazingly simple small cardboard butterflies from my handbag. I said, 'Put these in the side pocket of your backpacks. Every time your hand encounters the shape, remember, there is always a new day after the darkest night. Tomorrow, for all of you, a new beginning in the sunshine.'

I knew there was a miracle of grace when a girl called out, 'How did you *know* there were *thirty* of us?'

'I didn't!' I called back. 'I gave you all I had.'

It was a miracle indeed – the only butterflies left after weeks of journeying, thirty backpackers, thirty small shapes with sparkles on their wings. *Only God!* It was an *electric* moment, and I remember as I now write – the back section of that coach appeared to lighten as if *light* entered and diffused hopeless darkness.

We travelled many miles and detoured for hours until a hostel was located at a beach on the coast. It was able to house, feed, and accept *all* thirty young people. They would be safe, and some even later, I discovered, found permanent jobs. *Praise God!* I will always cherish the memory of gentle kisses and hugs as these young travellers exited the coach.

There were many more hours and many more delays before I too arrived back home. Gympie was now in full cleaning-up mode, and most shops were closed. David waited. I knew a warm bed, food, a shower, and a welcome from excited dogs all were at the end of this final journey. *It was all about Him.* I learnt the greatest life lesson. *Trust Him.* Follow the voice of only *the shepherd.*

The following stories are a sample only out of the whole time. I pray they will give a clear glimpse of the *butterfly journey.*

Man in a Cave

The entrance door to the small knick-knack shop was ghoulish. The doorframe had shark teeth images and what appeared to resemble spots of blood. Through glass could be seen massive shelves of dark skulls with glowing eyes. Halloween masks, weird symbols of ancient, modern, gothic, American Indian spirituality, exotic rugs, baskets, glitz, glitter, gloom, and trinkets of flashiness and 'bling-bling' were scattered everywhere.

I will not be going in there was my thought as I moved to walk right past.

'Yes. Go!'

The strong Spirit prompting made me stop. I entered with a shudder through the heavily beaded entrance.

A man sat alone in a chair behind a table. He looked up. 'You're the first person to come in here for two days,' he said.

'I came in to ask if you're OK.'

'Thank you for caring. In fact, I am not. I think I feel worse than I've ever felt in my life before.'

Without thought, I silently reached across and touched his shoulder. We both knew something happened. The oppressiveness in the room lifted. I knew it was God's presence. The man began to share. Together, as he spoke, we began to cry in a shared human bonding of deep grief and sorrow.

'I survived the Victorian bushfires,' he said, 'but I watched as friends, animals, properties, my business were all consumed by flames. I stood alone in a small, safe corner and wondered why I could not simply have died with everyone else.

'But restoration and healing came. I got myself out of the hole of despair and came to Queensland. Then my dad was killed by a drunken idiot when he was crossing a road. I moved further north alone to this beautiful little country town. I bought this business.

'The past few months have been incredibly happy. The people welcomed me, and lots of passing tourists brought a comfortable income and fun and laughter. Then these floods came. Images seared my mind. Folks around were all busy simply surviving. Grief overwhelmed me in waves. I was personally back in the bushfires traumatised in my mind.

'Once again, the thought as I sat here alone with all the roads closed – "What would it matter if I simply died too? Who would care? I could simply sit here and die." I was mulling this thought repeatedly in my mind. Then in you walked – a total stranger – and said, "How are you?" You touched my shoulder. *Wow!* I do not understand, but I don't feel alone anymore. It doesn't make sense.'

I felt in my bag, and the wing of a butterfly brushed my hand. I brought it out. It was beautiful (about fifteen centimetres in diameter). I placed it on the table in front of him. It had golden threads of sunlight shining across its wings.

I said softly, 'A symbol of love, hope, and new life.'

He clutched it in both his hands. 'Thank you, thank you. Oh, I feel love.' 'Divine love,' I said as I quietly left.

Through the window, I saw him holding the butterfly. Head bowed, he appeared to be praying. I silently prayed as I walked on.

Thanks be to God for His love, grace, and strength – in Jesus's name.
It's all about Him and His love.

Chemist Shop Woman

While walking in the street, I saw a woman leap out of a parked farm truck. She was dressed for farm work, and her laced boots were heavy – no frills, practical. She went into the chemist shop. She may have left a prescription.

I heard clearly the Spirit's voice – *Her!*

I entered the chemist shop and quietly walked up to the other woman.

'A little gift of love for you,' I said quietly. I handed her a butterfly. It was purple with little pearls down the centre.

'Oh my God! Thank you,' said the recipient. 'How did you know?'

All the girl assistants in the shop were mouthing silently to me,

'Thank you.' Other customers stood as if frozen.

'I know what it means,' the farm woman said. 'It is a symbol of divine Love, Hope, and new Life. What can I say but "thank you"?'

She began to cry, and so did everyone around. I quietly left in tears, also tearful but not knowing why.

About an hour later, the farm truck was further down the street when the young woman ran up to me.

'Thank you. You cannot possibly know what this means to me or how I know it *is* a message from *God*.'

No, indeed, I did not know. I did not need to know, but God surely *did*.

Thank You, my beloved Lord.

***

Tea Rooms

The outside sign read 'Tea Rooms'. Dainty lace cloths adorned scattered timber two- and four-seater tables. The inside was immaculate. There was no one in the street outside and no customers within. A young woman moved across the room towards me with her cupped hands stretched out as if in entreaty. Her lovely face was white and infinitely sad. ('Silver and gold have I none, but such as I do have, I give to you. In the name of Jesus Christ, be healed.' These words did not come to me until later.)

I had entered the room with two butterflies already in my closed hand –

117

two small purple identical butterflies. Gently and carefully, I placed one in each of her outstretched hands. She gasped and then smiled – a dazzling, radiant smile – and for an instant, she appeared to be bathed in light. We both stood very, very still. We were as if frozen.

I put my arms around her and softly said, 'I came to ask if you're OK.'

'I wasn't,' she said. 'I hadn't seen anyone all day. Without milk, I made a few black-only cups and pots of tea last week, but today not even my regulars are in town. No tourist buses – no people coming and going. No signs of life. It was like I had died. But *now* something is different. The butterflies are a sign of love and hope, aren't they?'

'And new life. Good times will return,' I added. 'Thank you! They are beautiful.'

I sat down and bought a cup of milkless coffee and shared with her a small plate of scones with jam. Before I left, we tearfully embraced. We were certainly aware of God's presence.

I departed a short time later. She waved at the door. Her smile was still radiant, and her face had lost its strain. She knew Jesus, and the reminder had jolted her back from sorrow into His healing embrace.

O Lord, water the seeds sown, and in Jesus's name, bring new life to this place, new life that is in You. Amen.

The Brass Butterfly

The overlander train enabled me to visit the remotest of inland Queensland towns. I came as an elderly 'visitor' and gently wandered and led by God, 'connected' with some in a deeper spiritual way. With most, I simply bought food or had coffees etc. This blessed them because *all* businesses were struggling with supplies.

The big brass butterfly, I carried at the bottom of my case – I do not remember if it was given or whether it was a purchase I made with donated funds – to aid a struggling hardware store. It was just there!

Sitting at a table with a group of locals in this large outback town (still cut off from the world and the rest of Australia except for the railway line), drinking water and homemade damper, I overheard some conversations about the problems the Mayor and his staff were experiencing – criticism, lack of staff, and not enough funding yet to restore infrastructure. Life was taking too long to get back to 'normal'. Some felt it was the Mayor's fault.

In my heart, I heard the Spirit say, *'Go to the City Hall.'*

I returned to my motel and brought out the brass butterfly and placed it and several other multicoloured butterflies in a light hold-all nylon bag.

'Two on sticks.'

This was inconvenient as the sticks protruded and made walking difficult, but the thought was insistent. These ones on sticks were weatherproof and for outside use.

I stood outside the city hall. It looked imposing, and I felt foolish in my simple clothing and sunhat. Inside, many desks were vacant. A few people were working in one small corner. They looked stressed, tired, and sad. At first, they did not even see me come in. One young man asked me politely if there was anything they could do to help me. A girl suggested that the salvos down the road still had some vouchers.

To my surprise, I spoke out strongly and clearly. 'I have something to give you.' I began to pass out a butterfly to each one and simply said, 'You may want to attach it to your desk. It is a reminder that you are loved. Better days are ahead.'

Smiles replaced sad expressions, and I went on to explain that all over Australia and many parts of the world, they were not forgotten. I was simply a carrier.

When I told them I had a gift for their mayor, one girl offered to escort me to his office. 'He needs right now someone who is giving, not asking for help. He is incredibly sad. A child in his immediate family died of leukemia at the height of the crisis. He has not had time to grieve. He has been overwhelmed by *everything*.'

He saw me walk in. I was aware of a young man, the same age as my eldest son. He rose from behind his desk, and I handed him the brass butterfly and, in simplicity. told him that prayers and love from many came with the simple gift.

He took it in his hands and silently bowed his head as if in prayer. 'I know what this symbol means. Tell the folk who sent it I know it is a message from the Lord on High. He knows us. We are not forgotten.

I will hang it on the back wall of my office.' It shone in his hands like a ray of golden light.

I left butterflies on the desks of staff who still could not get to work but who would soon return to busy, busy times. *Hope* for better will ever rise. I prayed with some in the foyer as I exited again into the street.

I shared butterflies and God's Love with many where I lunched on this day of surprises. I passed and repassed the Catholic primary school. I could not understand the drawing towards this place. They looked prosperous, and I could not believe they would lack anything.

I walked in, and the lady behind the desk (she looked like a nun – not in a habit but with a simple cross on her collar) enquired, 'My dear, has God directed you here?'

I was gobsmacked! 'All I have is two butterflies on sticks suitable for a garden. They are a simple gift if you would like them.'

Her eyes filled with tears. 'Please sit down, dear.'

Another woman came in, and the two, in an attitude of prayer, invited me to go with them to a small garden behind the preschool.

'When the flood was at its peak, one of our little preppies died. Her best friend has been grieving very much, and we suggested we would make a memorial tribute to her. She asked if butterflies could be a part of the memorial as Katie often spoke of seeing butterflies during her final days here on Earth with us. As symbols of new life promised by our Saviour, butterflies have become the way we will always remember her.'

I brought out the two butterflies on the garden sticks, and I was stunned, as they were, to see the shimmering, lovely glow on their coloured wings as sunlight reflected on the rain-proofed satin coating. They were beautiful!

'Do you mind if Katie's friend Josie comes out and joins us? I would like her to plant one in the garden as you do the same at the other end while we pray.'

I was too emotional to answer but nodded and smiled. It was a simple and holy moment. That little girl and I hugged with understanding of grief and loss. She smiled at me as she returned to class.

The time here was not yet finished. I was asked to return to the office.

The senior teacher asked me if I could prayerfully do something for her.

'Would you please visit the Mayor and share with him about the butterfly journey of hope? Katie was his loved niece, and her death has really shaken him.'

With *joy*, I told her of the brass butterfly, now on the Council Office wall. We went together into the chapel and thanked God for His miraculous hope and healing grace.

Amen. Thank You, Lord, for these memories as I write.

Two Angels in a Nursing Home Garden

An elderly man prayed with a group of others. They prayed for *all* who were cleaning up and for all who suffered loss or grief.

'Please, Lord,' he asked, 'could you give us a sign that we are not forgotten and You hear our prayers? Amen.'

Two nights later, as these seniors walked into their dining room, outside in the garden, he saw two angels. He called all the other residents, and this then became a night-time routine. Moonlight against the canopy of green leaves had cast a radiant light on two large white butterflies on stakes in their garden. Even in daylight, a nurse told me there was an almost *holy* light. Two large white butterflies on garden stakes had been my gift on behalf of Aglow Australia.

I went to this facility to visit my elderly cousin. I left the butterflies with the supervisor at the front desk. When I returned the following day to say goodbye to dear Elma (a passionate Christian), I heard the story of the two angels in the garden. I looked out on that garden in full sunlight, knowing they were *symbols* of new life found only in Christ, yet I could see a special light on their wings. I have come to believe that in this dark world, *divine love* lights up everything in His kingdom when hearts are pure.

The Dragonfly

The street was deserted but washed clean. There was now no sign of mud and destruction. Even the line of houses looked immaculate. Teams of dedicated folk had worked tirelessly to return their flood-damaged town to a semblance of normality. It would take months, but this street was complete. Sadly, the evacuated people had been taken to a variety of shelters, many in faraway towns. Most would not know they could now come home.

I walked this long street, attaching a butterfly to each mailbox (I was asked by a Salvation Army lass who assured me it would be valued) before I left. I realized a small boy was watching me from the end of the long street. He was standing beside his small scooter.

'Would you like to help?' I shouted. 'Better ask Mum,' I added.

His response sounded angry. 'Me mum's dead!' he shouted. 'And me dad's not back from his cleaning-up-mess job. He told me to play with my friends. None of them's back yet. They all got took away. I'm here waiting.' To my surprise, he suddenly pedalled down the footpath and stood beside me. 'Whatcha doin' anyway and why?'

'I'm putting butterflies on mailboxes to show the people God loves them and it is a new beginning for them.'

He laughed. 'I hate butterflies! I only like dragonflies. If God really loved me, He would send me a dragonfly.' Angry at life, he stood back and glared at me.

I remembered the mistake that was sent from a lady in Victoria. 'Perhaps God will use it,' she had said.

Please, Lord, help me to find it. I reached into my bag, and right at the bottom, my fingers encountered a slightly different shape, and I pulled it out. It was blue with coloured markings. The light touched it with a dazzling glow. It was a blue dragonfly with a clip to attach to a collar, a schoolbag, or the handlebars of a scooter. He gasped.

'God loves you,' I said gently.

He sobbed, and I embraced him. 'Please – can I help you?'

With his help, we completed every letterbox in his street. They all looked pretty and welcoming home. A bus arrived as I was walking away, but I heard children laughing and adults talking. I quietly walked back to my accommodation.

A vivid memory I will carry lifelong is of a small boy's stunned expression as he held in his hand not a butterfly but a significant dragonfly.

Amazing God! Amazing and miraculous is His love and grace.

Follow That Car!

I was walking the streets of this small town, saying hi to folks and generally being a 'visitor'. A car suddenly hurtled down the road. I moved onto the footpath. The car was a small blue/grey sedan driven by an extremely angry young woman. Her hair blew across her shoulders, and tendrils clung to the frame of the open window.

I heard the voice in my spirit. *'Follow that car.'*

My first response was *This is ridiculous. I feel like a spy or a stalker.* I tried to keep the car in sight and was pleased when I could see through the trees, where it stopped, and a clear view of the young woman. She unlocked a door and went into an upstairs apartment. I followed. I knocked on the door.

Her angry voice shattered the silence. 'Oh, go away. I am not interested in anything you are selling or any charity you are collecting for. *Go away!* I have nothing at all to give you. Leave me *alone!*'

I said quietly, 'I do not want anything. I was going to give you something.'

I now held in my hand a purple satin butterfly with silver on its wing tips. When she curiously opened her door a fraction, I shoved my hand through and placed it in her hand. She gasped.

The door opened fully, and when she scrutinised my senior person and was reassured I was safe, she politely enquired, 'Would like to join me for a cuppa? I would like a bit of company.'

The short time I spent with Sue (not her real name) only reinforced to me that in any disaster – be it flood, fire, earthquake, or other – the basic human need is for love and reassurance. If we have faith, God will move to sustain us. Sue's story was of loss and betrayal but, more serious than that, a loss of faith in Christ, which had been the wellspring of her life since childhood.

'I knew,' she said, 'when my parents died that God gave me great strength and was with me during the following years. Daniel arrived, and I believed he was God's blessing to me and joyfully planned a wedding and believed he would be with me forever. Two weeks before the planned wedding and one month before the worst flood in memory washed through here, Daniel phoned me and said he was leaving to work interstate but also the wedding was off, and Debbie was relocating with him. Debbie was to have been my bridesmaid. It was overwhelming, but my great job and my church family sustained me.

'The flood swept through town. Our church suffered massive damage, and most of the folks left town. I decided to stay. I was going to help but, as the waters rose, was advised "to stay home". One morning I saw struggling animals being washed away and, amid all the loss and heartache, felt the bottom drop out of my own world. I know it was delayed grief, but the loss of the belief in God was the catalyst. Hopeless despair took over. If there is no God, then there is no hope for any of us. I longed to be swept away in the flood as well.

'The rain stopped. The water went down, but somehow I had died inside. A hand fluttered inside my door, and a satin butterfly was in my hand. My grandfather's voice from years ago came back to me – "Child, keep looking up! Like a butterfly is a symbol of life, God reveals Himself in mysterious ways."'

We talked a lot. I shared with her about my own nine days before the wedding abandonment story, and we then talked about faith and how real the voice of the shepherd had proven to be for me in recent weeks. We talked about butterflies and her now renewed hope for a future.

We prayed together, and she encouraged me by saying, 'If you had only come to my town and spoken to me, I believe God's purposes would have been fulfilled. I thank God for you, and I thank you.'

Thank you, my blessed Saviour!

A Final Storm A large inland Queensland town is surrounded by vast open land stretching as far as the eye can see. Huge river plains – *desolation*. Fences are all gone, animals washed away. Many homestead houses are still standing, but until all the rivers recede, only helicopters can drop supplies and search for life among the dead.

A man stood staring at the wide expanse of open street. He leant against a telegraph post. I stood beside him and put my hand on his arm.

'You OK, mate?' I gently enquired.

He knew I was a visitor and a stranger. He gulped and, as his voice broke, replied, 'No, I am not. This is the corner where my son Billy, only 8 years old, fell and was trampled to death by a frightened horse. That was twenty years ago.'

He began sobbing in deep, heart-wrenching gasps. He allowed me to hold him in a tight embrace.

'I am sorry,' I whispered softly.

'I thought I had dealt with the grief years ago. Oh! Why? Why has it all come back so vividly? This massive flood. My cattle washed to the sea, fences vanished – and I am thankful that my wife and family members were safely rescued from our barn roof. Here I am, safe and dry, supposed to be helping with the clean-up/ Here I am! Paralysed by a twenty-year-old vivid memory. Why? Why?'

I had no answer. I stood beside him and held him. He cried, and I found I cried as well. We shared in deep grieving. I have no idea how long we stood there. I often wonder if passers-by noticed. Silence came.

He said, 'Thank you for listening, and thank you for caring. I will get back to cleaning.'

I handed him two small butterflies to put in his back pockets.

His radiant face stunned me. 'I'll give them to my wife. She has always told me, "Symbols of *life* and *hope* restore the soul." Thank you for visiting us here.'

I handed him an envelope of stickers. 'For the children at the rescue centre.' I prayed as he walked away, *Thank You, my Lord, for making it all possible. Amen.*

'Amen! Amen!' I was not aware I had prayed aloud, but I heard responses from somewhere in the street.

That night, I walked to the local pub. Pub meals were still thriving. I ordered a steak. What came out on my plate would have fed a family. I kept what I could eat and placed the rest on a communal centre table platter. Many of these burly hard-working cattle men relished the idea of *seconds.*

A huge TV across the back wall began showing graphic images of the Christchurch earthquake. This main quake followed the minor disturbance of a few weeks before. This was *devastation.* These resilient men immediately focussed on 'our cousins across the ditch' – a term for New Zealanders.

'Maybe we could suggest the kids in the shelter prepare a package for kids over there. We're in a hell of a mess here, but those b——s over there are in for a rough trot.'

Memories . . . memories . . . memories! Perhaps they made and sent butterflies – I really do not certainly know. I only *know* my God is in the whole tragedy of human existence until His Kingdom comes.

Later, twenty thousand butterflies were sent to a pastor in Japan who appealed to a former exchange student living in Victoria, Australia.

'What can I possibly sow to bring hope to my people overwhelmed and destroyed in life by this tsunami?'

She sent him the butterflies, which he prayerfully scattered over all the destruction. The people returned to find nothing left of their town, but butterfly symbols were on rocks, wedged in tree roots – everywhere. Smiles replaced tears, and young folks collected them. However, when the *real* butterflies soared back even before their destroyed town was fixed, the people appreciated and understood the pastor's passionate sermon.

'In Christ alone is found *life everlasting*. He lived and died as a sacrifice to save your souls but rose again to show you all His promise of *eternity*.'

Amen

CHAPTER 22

2011–2020

Personal Hills and Valleys

Health events as I aged (I would have preferred not to have journeyed through) have become valuable lessons of who God, in the valleys of my own life experiences, really is.

At the end of 2011, before the incredible flood year ended, my valleys began. It is not my intention to record the medical details of these events but to explain that it was a bit like dodging bowling balls. Nothing took me out, but sometimes I journeyed where I did not want to go and met many people along the way who did not survive and went 'home'.

In September and October 2011, I was in hospital on three separate occasions because of a positive breast cancer diagnosis. The shock during this time was worse than the operations. The apparently non-invasive nature of my cancer was hopeful, but two dear friends had died in the early years of the twenty-first century, so all the drama of cancer support networks and meeting of so many on the way who had far more life-threatening futures was a learning curve as well as a valley. The worry – and I was constantly being reminded – was that I would have secondary cancers in other parts of my body.

I can affirm – I give thanks to my God. I was aware of *His presence always in and on the way.* One event during a specific operating theatre journey remains with me. I had farewelled David back in my hospital room. I knew he would pray.

I was wheeled into a pre-surgery room where in pristine, blue-covered theatre trolleys, six of us were lined up, waiting. A couple of anxious husbands were allowed to stay with their teary wives, and it was their distress which triggered a humorous response from me. *Only God..*

Brightly and cheerfully, I said, 'Well, here we are, gathered together, anonymous and all journeying in one direction. When they collect us to deliver us into the hands of our surgeons, we have been told bits of us will be removed. Let us now settle back and wait our turn. As long as we *know* and they *know* which bits to remove ... all will be well. Life may be different after, but every breath of life matters. As long as they do not remove our heads, we'll be OK.'

For some reason, everyone laughed, and one of the husbands called from the door as he left, 'You tell 'em, ladies – they must not remove your heads!'

This bit of silliness lightened the room, and we had time to then share a little of our stories. Young Susan, whose family had a long history of breast cancer, had chosen to have a complete mastectomy when diagnosed with breast cancer at only 25. Her Mum had died at 40. She had been terrified. Her operation could protect her life from this form of the disease.

All our stories were different. For some, it was a first time for biopsy, and this result could be life-changing but ever *hopeful* for them. This was my third time, and the outcome would be 'uncertain'. I was prepared for a breast removal but had confidence in my surgeon's wisdom and expertise. I also put my trust in the *One* who would direct my life's journey till His purposes were fulfilled. I had confidence that I would not upset anyone if I said a gentle prayer as each trolley was rolled away.

We all kept hearing soft laughter coming from the operating theatre. I was called as number five this morning, and two brightly smiling attendants came to wheel me away.

My gowned and masked surgeon said as I entered, 'You're the one. I should have known. Every woman this morning has announced brightly, 'Do not remove my head!' What do you have to say for yourself?'

'Please do not remove my head!'

As I drifted off to sleep under the anaesthetic, I remember hearing a nurse remark, 'This has been an unexpectedly peaceful, almost joyful morning.'

Each woman, when she returned to her hospital bed, would find a beautiful lace butterfly on her bedside table. I thank the husbands who, without understanding, gently placed them there. Again, it is all about *Him.* As I was packing, there was a gentle spiritual nudge: '*Pack six beautiful symbols of grace and peace.'* The sixth butterfly was given to the young woman carer waiting in the foyer for her mum to come out.

I was leaving with David. My results had been good. It was believed that surgery had removed *all* malignant cells. The area was not extensive and did not appear to be invasive in nature. My breast was returned to a relatively normal appearance – clever reconstruction with eventual *settling.* My gratitude to God was not about *externals* but for my life and the hope to live it for Him.

It was recommended that David and I speak with a professor of oncology (cancer specialist), a dear friend of my surgeon. It was a miracle to get to speak with this dear man who was able to talk openly with us as a couple about the way forward – all the 'things that *could* happen' and the possibilities of a long, uneventful life. He agreed with us that more radical protective surgery was 'overkill'. He understood our desire to place our lives and our futures completely into God's hands. I agreed to monitor carefully checks on all aspects of caring for my temple. Thus continued the journey.

Hills and valleys indeed!

CHAPTER 23

Writing– Inspiration– God's Gift

I t would be impossible to journey onwards through the hills and valleys of life after the butterfly journey of 2011 without mentioning the wonderful and joyous years of writing inspiration in the middle *of it all*. It was almost as if the possibility of not living long enough to completely use what He inspired fuelled me to express it all in written form.

The journey has been as vast as the ocean, but always, the heartbeat of faith resonated. The bear stories became fully a part of the whole. On the website I still maintain – www.golden-rains.com – this is where all the bear stories remain, including some info regarding my life and my journey. However, *Shafts of Gold* is the *memoir* endeavouring to tie the rich tapestry of the whole life together. An amazing God who is still answering a small child's big question – 'Do you exist? *Who are you*? *Really?*'

Beyond the Ashes is an Australian story with a theme about the power of forgiveness, never meant to be a novel of prominence. God did not make me a great crafter of clever phrases etc. I am a storyteller, and these are the stories that I needed to tell in my lifetime. Though fiction, all the people and their lives are *real* to me. I feel and live with and for them. *Beyond the Ashes*, in places, tore at my heart, and the people remain family.

I am thankful for helpful people in writing groups and advice given to me about online resources and possibilities. Becoming a WordPress blogger remains, for me, both a joy and a goal each day. I prayerfully consider my own blog, Passionate Creative Christian, and ask for *His* inspiration twice weekly. I love 'connecting' with bloggers worldwide. They inspire and challenge me.

It was at a university writer's week that a lecturer wanted to speak with me personally. (I had been sponsored by the local council in my town of Gympie. I was delighted to attend and inspired by my time there.)

The tutor Paul spoke earnestly with me about whether I wrote longer stories than what we were doing during this seminar. 'I like what you have written here but believe you have longer works within you that you will express. Have you ever thought about a story set in your own community?'

I had never considered another long story after *Ashes* but discovered, when I returned home, his words germinated in my mind. It took research and consultations with the library and an Aboriginal advisor, but eventually, I put pen to paper, and *Marranga-Limga* became a reality. This historically accurate story about fictional people came alive through the years as personal events (like the little girl found in an alley behind the pub) were discovered to have archival records of accuracy. After *Marranga-Limga*'s completion, I had it published in book form.

In my heart, even as health issues swirled, was this certainty there was more to this story. I had to write on to 'What happened next?' This question became complex when, during research, world interest was aroused by revelations hidden because of wartime secrecy. Truth was uncovered from both the First and Second World Wars, with graves of missing soldiers also being discovered. I could then write with historical accuracy about my fictional family into a truly remarkable, if sad and at times difficult to express, *future*. *Legacy of Limga* became this book.

Two meditation books – *Peace* and *Our God Lives!* – came about when I compiled, from my previously published mediations in the Upper Room, a selection. These were published at the same time as the last two books as a financial incentive to me to publish the two Gympie stories.

All the books have been beautifully published, but I have received extremely meagre royalties as all are too highly priced and few folks are interested even in e-books when the market is flooded with inexpensive literature. I have never been able to afford expensive marketing for any books. He inspired – their future is His business. I surrendered to *Him*, I really only wanted *His* presence in my life, to be acknowledged about God through His giftings.

Two *Peace meditation* books found homes, one on a cancer waiting room table and the other in a hospital waiting room. Hard covered, they looked stunning in full colour as table books of A3 size. My joy and thanks to God was for being able to give them as gifts to these facilities. May it be only *God! All about Him!*

CHAPTER 24

Life's Bowling Balls

T he next few years for me, in retrospect, were a bit like tenpin bowling, Stuff whirled, and although the ball *hit* (I believe, because of the grace of God), *nothing* took me *out*.

There were many *high points*. I attended conferences with incredible spiritual encouragement. My attendance was mostly by miraculous provision, which stunned people without understanding and faith. It was as if God continued to teach and train me to really *know Him*.

I went twice to Orlando in Florida, USA, and both times there, I encountered on the flights or at the conference people of faith who influenced me or who told me encountering me had brought about in them a strengthening of faith. Two men remain indelibly etched in my mind.

Both were moved mid-flight to sit in seats either side of me. I was in a seat in the evacuation chute row. Extra leg room was given to me because of the necessity to stretch out my swollen knee. They were both big men crammed in small seats and were moved to provide physical strength in the event of a crash. We were travelling from Dallas to Brisbane, a non-stop twenty-three-and-a-half-hour journey.

During severe storms, we were asked by a steward if we would pray. Together, in silence, we connected with God. These men did not know each other, but we three formed immediately a strong spiritual bond. Both men were on missionary journeys to different parts of the world, one to Papua New Guinea and the other to China (he was to connect with a team in Sydney). We said, 'Good evening' and settled down to rest.

One suddenly said to me, 'Where have you been?' The other interjected. 'Your face is glowing.'

I began to share about the conference. They were astonished by some of the teaching and encouraged me to share more. Our rest intentions were forgotten. We talked about the need to *die to self* so that God would be the leader and total force for *all* of our life's endeavours and challenges.

'*Are you dead yet?*' was the spiritual challenge we all faced. It was to them back in the early 2000s and must be, for all of us through life, powerful teaching. Unless the self is *crucified* with Christ and we are *born again in the Spirit*, God can never minister as *who* He is to others in power and fullness.

We talked a lot that night. I learned a lot of rich Bible scholarship, and together, when we safely disembarked, we *knew* God had arranged our meeting. We had been ignited by the experience. When the cabin crew sat opposite us as the plane came into land, they asked to know what we had been sharing. They said we all *glowed*. We passionately shared, and God the Holy Spirit moved on them. When they too disembarked, in some inexplicable way, they appeared *changed* as well. Only God!

Because of Aglow International, I attended many inspirational and life-enhancing conferences. I passionately longed to see denominational barriers disappear in my hometown, but even today, in some areas there is furious clinging to 'old ways . . . old wineskins', as the parable taught. I went to gatherings in all states in Australia and had astonishing encounters with First Nation Christians both in Uluru and Adelaide.

Visionary gifts of God continued to inspire me, and always, my relationship with Christ led me onwards. In Vanuatu, I had the privilege of sleeping on grass mats. I saw firsthand the beauty of island life and, more than that, the passion of their Christian heralding of each new day, with the abundant *joy* of worshipping their Saviour. Here is an insert from my diary.

Vanuatu Calling

On a beach in Caloundra in 2014, during an Aglow conference there, I was aware of God's presence and a profound certainty of His plans and purposes for the Great South Lands of the Holy Spirit. For me, this was deep and impacting.

I heard and spiritually saw 'Vanuatu in the clouds. To this, I surrendered and prayed. 'Lord, if You are calling, I will go, but please guide and supply my needs to go.' He did, and the calling was miraculously confirmed when, before the next day's meeting, Gloria from Vanuatu met me in the foyer.

She said, 'God told me to wait here, and I would know.*' She walked towards me and said, 'I would like to invite you to attend the Kingdom Calling Conference, to be held in Vanuatu.'*

I knew Aglow and our dear Kerry-Ellen were going. There were plans to establish Aglow there. I could never fully explain – I was Aglow, and because of Aglow, I accepted to go. However, it became for me a life-changing personal journey.

I stayed with Gloria, her husband, and their children in their home – hut – before the conference started, where I also participated in bucket shower facilities and, outside, very basic toilet provisions. This was a learning experience, and the richness of Christian worship more than compensated for my 70-year-old Western ideals of life. It was magnificently inspirational.

I shared a hut with the Vanuatuan women during the conference and slept on a mat on the ground. These four days were awe-inspiring. Their children danced and worshipped God early each day on the beach. The husbands praised Him with the dawn, and the men's hut shook with their passion and love. A shaking one night – 'Oh, an earthquake! God is speaking. We must pray and worship.' We then did! It was here in the conference I met Alpha from the Solomon Islands and the husband-and-wife pastors from New Caledonia.

I can only describe my connection with everyone as miraculous and of the Spirit. *They called me Mumma Sarah. All I can ever explain is we were one in the Spirit. I eventually adapted to different food, the long uphill walk to the toilet each night, and the fact that there seemed to be no time in Vanuatu . . . Things just happened. Some mornings, I simply lay around until I was taken for a swim (a warm bucket shower in an enclosed hillside hut facility). Meals happened, and the beginning of a conference also just happened. Learning was joyous as well as, at times, difficult.*

I was unexpectedly invited to speak on the morning the Prime Minister walked in. Unprepared, I simply shared my vision in the washing machine in the 1980s when I first knew *that Australia and the islands of the South Pacific had a unique part to play in God's coming Kingdom.*

Spiritually, I have often felt isolated as an intercessor but always joined with Christ for all. I do sincerely thank God for Aglow. This ministry has always spiritually cemented my life.

***

Aglow's ministry expanded my thinking and understanding of other faiths and their darkness and of the penetrating *light* of Christ beginning to beam everywhere. Cultures, skin colour, and racial divide had to disappear when the sacrifice at the cross was understood to *encompass* all human souls.

Across the vastness of the great south lands of the Holy Spirit and the wonder of all the massive continents and rich lifestyles, in my life journey of clear insight into the realm of spiritual darkness, I was continuing to grow. I was still only gradually comprehending my understanding of *who* God the Holy Spirit really is. I was able to clearly see that despite rising social discord and political correctness, there is only *one way* to eternity, *one Saviour* for all souls, *one* blood-drenched sacrificial cross for us *all*. This was forming as rock-solid faith as my life journey through valleys of health issues continued.

2014

After a few discomforting but minor experiences in early 2014 and my feeling tired after an inspirational conference, an abdominal scan revealed a malignant womb tumour. The big question swirling was being asked – 'Is this a secondary to breast cancer?'

In early December, after a full-body MRI and careful checks for cell changes in all vital organs, I went to hospital and underwent a full hysterectomy – no real loss to an elderly lady but physically weakening, I discovered.

The anaesthetist later told me he lost my pulse after the op and said to the surgeon, 'I think we may have lost her.'

He told me from the table, I said clearly, 'No! *I'm still here.*' Everything being monitored then returned to normal.

Christmas 2014 was both a celebration of our Lord's birth and personally a celebration of *life* and the gift of *hope* He gives to all. That Christmas Day, I spent quietly lounging but enjoyed grandchildren and the *joy* of the season – a beautiful summer day and a beach visit as well. Family support! *Life! Love! Laughter!*

The year 2015 was a quiet year health wise, but physically, I was becoming 'less able'. After anaesthetics, I seem to become weaker. The world situation was rapidly changing and societies experiencing an overturn of God-fearing respect for life and Biblical standards and God and relationship with Christ being pushed behind issues of people's rights, climate change, and all issues relating to 'self' or perceived injustice. I still attended wonderful inspirational conferences, and spiritual life, writing life, and family life journeyed on.

In 2016, walking became painful, and I experienced sharp heel pains. Plantar Fascilitis was diagnosed with many recommended exercises. For me, the rolling under my foot arch of a frozen bottle of water while softly singing 'Jesus Loves Me' and 'Row, row, row your boat gently down the stream' helped lessen the heel pain. Now with special shoes, sandals, and thongs, all with slight heel support, I walk easily and more swiftly. Registering with Home Help assisted with the installation of handrails and other minor adjustments to make our simple home safer for folk getting *older.*

Throughout 2016, I began to experience strange 'passing out' events, not frequent but unexpected. On one memorable evening, our son announced his engagement at the dinner table. I had just sliced a piece off my fillet steak and reached over to savour the portion. I felt suddenly strange and gently slid into unconsciousness. It was brief, but unable to move, I sat where I was. Our son suspected it was a stroke. The cheerful paramedics reassured me on our trip to hospital this was *not* the case. I remember my feeling of gratitude. After this trip to hospital, I was subjected to several tests which revealed nothing of significance. I did not renew my driving licence, and we became a onecar couple. Life rolled on.

In October 2016, I was again taken to hospital by ambulance and admitted. As I settled back again in the emergency section bed in the Gympie Hospital, I was aware of this feeling of *well-being* and no *anxiety.* I began to wonder, as no doubt others were, if I was having panic attacks or a problem of food allergies or even if it was a mental condition.

Once I was in the bed and being monitored, there were no problems evident. Heart, blood pressure, and *all* vital checks, including -rays, were normal. I looked smiling and well. I felt relaxed and felt in the peak of health as well. (I was aware of God's presence with me.)

My appearance was vastly different to when the paramedics picked me up at home. I was usually very pale. I always found that 'drifting out' in a semi-faint, often with chest pains and nausea, made me incapable of moving. The signs were all there, I was told, for either stroke or heart attack.

A relief female doctor who had seen me once after I had almost passed out because of extended standing during a mammogram came to see me just before the evening meal. She asked if I would be prepared to travel by ambulance to the hospital supervised by a university contemporary of hers who was a specialist in his field. He had a room unexpectedly available, and I could be taken there *straight away* (a miracle when appointments to see specialists often took weeks).

I had a delightful hour-long journey with two young paramedics who were keen to talk with me about faith, life, and the joy of living. They ensured I was hooked up to a whole array of monitoring devices, and I believe they too marvelled that we had so much fun as we travelled. It was a joyful experience! *Only God!*

The beautiful private room I was settled into took my breath away. It was not like a hospital here but more like a holiday room. I accepted it as a God blessing. I was welcomed by a smiling Dr Lim, who is a specialist cardiologist. He supervised my connection to an array of monitoring devices. Then he ordered a thoroughly enjoyable dinner. I settled down after enjoying this to a peaceful night's sleep.

Before dawn, the silence was shattered by the return of an elated, smiling Dr Lim. 'I've found it! I have found it! I've got it. Your heart rhythm is healthy and strong, but I detected the faintest *skip* if your blood pressure goes down or when you are shocked or excited. Once in the night, the merest *flutter* while you were dreaming. You are an extremely fortunate lady. It is minor. It is fixable. You can be guarded from harm by having the newly perfected Boston Scientific Pacemaker inserted. It will keep your heart and you safe for the rest of your life.

There is a team of experts now worldwide who are trained. I can do this op later today. I have a team and theatre available. You are a fortunate lady indeed!'

I did not feel fortunate. I was shocked – a device placed *inside* me to remain always. When I phoned and spoke with David, he was grateful that a diagnosis had been found and was encouraging and supportive. Dr Lim came and discussed with me the procedure.

'Do I *have* to have a general anaesthetic?' I asked.

'Yes.' He looked at me intently. 'There is an alternative of a gentler option but not one I recommend. It is usually better for us all if the patient is unconscious.' He however agreed to trial my request.

More settled in my spirit, I prayed, *Heavenly Father, please be with us all. Amen.*

Travelling on the trolley to the theatre early in the afternoon was bouncy; sunlight filtered through the large windows along the corridor as we travelled. An unexpected feeling of joy washed over me. I laughed.

The startled hospital orderly grinned and said, 'You are the happiest person I have seen today.'

'Not me,' I replied. 'But I do believe the *joy* of the Lord is my strength.'

He wanted to know more, so I told him about my Heavenly Father and His Comforter, who is my internal best friend.

***

I am not certain if what I said made sense as I was, like a child, only learning myself. I had come to accept simply He was more awesome than I ever imagined and learned to surrender to His grace.

The operation began. I was told an anaesthetist was standing by to render me unconscious if I grabbed his hand. I breathed deeply and closed my eyes. I settled back and knew I was totally relaxed.

In my imagination, I walked towards a beautiful green grassy paddock. 'Oh!' I said aloud. 'I see a black horse with a white mane.'

'What did she say?' one of the assistants asked.

Dr Lim then spoke to me. 'Faye, will you speak a little louder, please? Tell us *all* of what you are seeing. I have not witnessed this before, but it is as if you are on a journey and have a story to tell. Please continue.'

I see a vibrant green paddock with trees shimmering in the distance and all along the sides. A black horse gallops in. His main is purest white and flowing in the wind. He paws at the air and then begins a gallop, increasing to lightning speed as he circles the paddock. It is like a paddock dance *of exultant joy.*

A palomino gallops in. Ripples of golden light catch and reflect the sunlight. She tosses her head and turns to greet two new arrivals. A grey mare with a small chestnut foal frolicking at her heels are now entering the paddock. There is a resonating sound of joyful neighed greetings.

I see a massive piebald stallion. He stops. Is he perhaps a guarding presence for them all? He neighs a strident greeting, and then as he is joining them, they together prance, almost dance, and then gallop round and round the paddock. It is a joyous exhibition of freedom, colour, and life.

A gentle wind stirs the grass. Beautiful! Beautiful! Beautiful! How beautiful this scene is!

***

The voice of Dr Lim penetrated my thoughts. 'It is all finished,' he said. 'The operation is *over*. It went *extremely well*.'

What an amazing experience! Without understanding of why or how, I only affirm my certainty that it was *God!* From the hospital theatre staff, it was shared as the most 'enjoyable' operation any of them had ever attended. Through the years, Dr Lim has not forgotten and always affirms *it was supernatural and amazing. Amazing God!*

Following the pacemaker implant, there were three minor incidents of my fainting – all occurred at times of pressure or hurry when I knew I should have sat down or rested for a period. Every time someone benefitted by seeing the new technology in this device and the experiences were times when I knew the swift care and response from the doctors who understood Boston Scientific data etc. Very minute adjustments were made. My problem was an occasional heart skip. This device was a bit hypersensitive to minor heart changes, but now I do not even know it is there, and that aspect of who I am is sorted. Praise *God!*

Even when David and I travelled to Melbourne to see his aunt for her 95th birthday in 2017 and had a great time with family and hospitable cousins, I spent a night in hospital – one of the pacer glitches - because I tried to see and do too much. It helped staff and doctors to understand the new technology. I found out later they did not charge us for my care because of what they learnt. Memories of that time and one night in Casey Hospital remain precious memories.

***

Memories too of a Happy, Holy Christmas in 2016

CHAPTER 25

2017 — Disturbance on the Sea

I have no understanding of the whys during these two years, but I can affirm my certainty that *God was with us* even if, at times, we did look upwards and moan a little about life journey hiccups.

The year 2017 began with a feeling of life travelling along with only minor bumps on the road. As we aged, there were more tests for hearing, eyesight, and the general maintenance of our bodies. We saw folks younger than ourselves leaving this life through illness or accident and were grateful for our lives and our faith.

Before summer returned and Christmas joy enriched us, both David and I had to go to hospital for surgery. It was a shock when a routine bowel test revealed David had a four-centimetre cancerous polyp. It was after his op, and with a few glitches as his body returned to relatively normal – with now, for him, a need for yearly check-ups – I was told of another bowling ball of life heading my way.

I was with him at his check-up visit and was a bit surprised when the surgeon wanted to speak with me. I had wondered why the appointment had been made for us *both*. Again, I would be hit, but His grace deflected from what could have been worse.

***

After *five years of clear results* and ongoing maintenance tests, the *shock* diagnosis after my October mammogram revealed a malignant twenty-millimetre tumour in my right breast. It again did not show indications of rapid spread, but its appearance shocked the doctor. It certainly *shocked* me! *Why, Lord, when I thought all the dramas were behind me?*

The operation to remove the tumour and the main lymph gland from under my armpit took place on December 22. The wonderful news came that the lymph gland had shown a totally *negative* result. No malignant cells had escaped into the bloodstream.

The decision was made to again restore the breast instead of removing it. Radiation was recommended to destroy any inside rogue cells. I was told that for the type of tumour I had, removal of the breast was not recommended because tumours could attach to breast bones with easier access to internal organs. My breasts, in fact, were a kind of protective armour for my insides. This thought amused me – a little bit mangled but still with a purpose.

The anaesthetist spoke with me before the op. He remembered me from the 2014 theatre incident when my pulse seemed to disappear. He promised he was going to monitor me carefully, especially now that I had the pacemaker. The operation went exceptionally well.

'The pacemaker was brilliant,' this doctor told me later. 'It kept everything flowing in perfect rhythm.'

I know I felt great afterwards and even wanted dinner that same evening. I gave thanks to the Lord for my blessings.

Christmas 2017 was a joyous family time. Both Dave and I rejoiced that we both were still here, maybe with many more years ahead.

Happy birthday remembrance to Christ the Saviour *King*!

***

2018

This new year began with a fresh connection on the phone, with the McGrath Foundation nurse who had journeyed with me through the initial breast cancer scare of 2012. She was surprised and a little shocked that we had met once again. Several women both young and older had died since we first met. Many others like me had been presumed healed by surgery and gone on with their lives. Here again I was. Why?

Wonderful support came in the mail from the Breast Cancer Care Team. I received a beautiful diary, a free bra with support panels, and a sheaf of new help pamphlets and health tips etc. – nothing at all about spiritual needs. Thank God I knew the *one* who would supply that.

The *radiation journey* began 22 January 2018. What a journey this turned out to be – hills of soaring heights and valleys, but what a rich dimension to life this became! What memories!

After all the initial tests and the complex marking of the targeted radiation area, I was welcomed to the Genesis family, which comprised all recent patients who would begin their radiation journey. The clinic is called Genesis ('new life'), and men and women needing cancer treatment were treated like members of a social club. We all were issued with trendy blue carry bags which held folders of details of each person's individual medical files, appointments, allergies, etc.

Indeed, in that place, we became family. For the ones who also had chemo, it was valuable indeed that we connected each day and often shared a cuppa and a laugh before treatments began. Because of a few of us living in another town, an even smaller (only six of us) family formed. We were transported daily in a Cancer Care minibus. Stopping on the way, we had three to pick up. If someone was ill and unable to come, it saddened us all. We heard later that one had died. It was like we had lost a friend!

My treatment was twenty-one days. This was broken by weekends and one public holiday but quite a strain for David as he travelled twice a day from our home in the hinterland to deliver me to the bus and then pick me up when I returned about four hours later. It was an exhausting time for us both.

I know in retrospect, I remember each day that I returned home, I was hungry and travel weary and wanted nothing else but to sleep or to float on the top of our wading pool. It was summer and extremely hot. My radiated breast always felt like it conducted its own heat as well. This was the background to a wonderful God adventure that inspired my life and, I earnestly pray, impacted others to seek for the only *one* who is a God of *personal presence* and anointing.

The second day in the clinic, a young woman sat down beside me. She was crying.

'I don't want to do this,' she said. 'I would rather die.'

Her husband came to sit with us. 'Please, could you do something to help her? She hates confined places and is sure being enclosed in a small cylinder will kill her.'

I hugged the young woman and said quietly, 'Peace, dear one. I have had two treatments so far and know that you must fix your mind on something beautiful, close your eyes, and think *only* on that. It really will be all right.'

I did not add that because I was praying, I did not have to worry about what images I was thinking about. He was my companion. I was about to gently introduce her to my friend, but she burst into tears again and spoke.

'What can I fix my mind on? I'm so scared. Everything seems hopeless.'

In that instant, I believe God inspired me, and this then began, even for me, a wonderful journey of discovery.

I said to her husband, 'Please, will you pass over to us one of the magazines from the table over there?' I handed the book to Marianne

(I found out her name later) and said, 'Go through this book and find a beautiful image and think only of this. Picture it in your mind. Forget the sounds and keep your eyes closed. Let only the image be your focus.'

She happily chose her image and was wheeled away for her treatment, smiling. I began to quietly pray. It was only when her husband wanted me to know what picture she had chosen that my prayer became more urgent. Marianne had chosen a massive plate of assorted foods as her 'something beautiful'. On the other page beside the food was the picture of a pathway leading to the sea in the distance. I loved it, and it became the image I focussed on that day.

Marianne returned just as I was being wheeled to the treatment room. She looked happy and excited.

'Thank you!' she called. 'I had no problems. It went well, and I have worked out several new recipes to add to my collection. I was well looked after, but I remember now more about ingredients than what was occurring around me. I saw all the ingredients clearly on the picture in my mind.'

Oh, Lord, thank you. Journey with her in the days ahead and reveal Yourself in the process. Amen. I had told her husband of my faith in Jesus when he saw me praying. I did not meet up with them again but often was reminded to pray for them in the weeks ahead.

As I entered the radiation room for my third treatment and greeted the young nurse attendants, I told them of the image I had chosen to mindfully look at during the procedure. It was a spontaneous sharing with them; I had not planned it, but their enthusiasm to know what would happen inspired me.

The image of the path and its winding curve towards the sea was beautiful to think about. I began to walk onwards as the road continued. The ocean still appeared very distant. It seemed like the path would never end. Along the edges were native flowers and clumps of silvery grasses. In my imagination, as I continued walking, I enjoyed looking at the various colours in the wildflowers and appreciated that although they mostly grew in sandy soils, their colours and variety were stunningly beautiful.

Suddenly, there was a stand of trees, and between the trees, the blue of the ocean sparkled in the distance. I burst through the trees, and the panorama of sand and sea caused me to gasp with pleasure. How I now longed to walk along the pristine sands!

'It's finished,' the radium nurse said. 'One more treatment is now behind you.'

She probably thought I was a bit batty when I replied, 'Another five minutes, and I would have been walking on the hard sand.'

The next day, I did indeed walk along the beach. What glorious memories of the next two days and my carefree beach walks, which I still hold dear! Thank God indeed – how He brings His peace into all circumstances in His unique way for us as individual children!

(On my fourth treatment, I was left with a slightly burnt area, but even this hiccup on the way did not destroy how He inspired me to journey through it *all*.)

The Beach Walk

Many events occurred as the days unfolded, and I was surprised that not just the nurses but also many of the doctors and support people asked me, 'What happened today?'

Out of one journey, I later wrote a short story. I was paddling in a canoe. *That was my picture.* Suddenly, in my story, I fell out, and the canoe drifted away, and I climbed a tree and waited for rescue. The story I later wrote is called 'The Drifting Canoe'.

The image of an iceberg in Antarctica began the last journey I will share. Among many others I have recorded in a diary, this one stands out because I *know* it was God who led me through the noise and medical inertia, and I went where I did not even know in the natural sense.

One of the care nurses came to see me in the waiting Area. 'Where are you going today, Faye?'

I showed her the image. 'I'm going to Antarctica.' The image in the travel brochure was of a bleak, barren ice flow. It looked remote and very cold.

She shivered. 'What are you going to see and do there?'

'I have no idea. I will let you know when I return from the treatment.'
'Please, will you share with us? The whole team is extremely interested.'

I promised, without any certainty I would see more than ice and clear blue sky. If I relaxed, their job – and my journey – would flow smoothly.

The usual preparations and safety precautions were checked and double-checked, and encased in the cylinder once more, I was rolled in. I breathed in deeply and spiritually took my Father in heaven's hand.

I stood on the ice and looked up at the extraordinary expanse of blindingly blue sky. Then I walked forward. I accepted this as normal even though I had no visible sign of warm clothing or any practical helps. I moved and began to walk quite swiftly across an expanse of glacial ice until I reached a cliff face with an open cave-like entrance.

I entered the cave, and what I saw was breathtakingly beautiful. The inside was a blue cavern, and the ice was shimmering with a special warmth. There was light, and the whole cavern seemed to resonate with hope *and God's presence.*

I knew the treatment was finished when a puzzled voice said, 'I think she's asleep.'

'No, I'm not.'

Five people gathered to hear whether I had journeyed anywhere. I shared the story. They were amazed!

When I returned the following day, I had printed out an amazing picture I found and gave them all a copy in a coloured envelope. The image I discovered was exactly what I had seen. It came from a science site where someone believed there were blue ice caverns in Antarctica.

A comment below the site with the image I have copied (free of copyright) added that this was what someone claimed could be seen – but rarely. It is what I saw on my journey. For me, this remains a d*ivine, holy, and sacred memory*.

Thank you, Amazing Lord!

A Cherished Reminder of a Journey

2018 Continues

I longed for a peaceful recovery time for my body to be restored. I found I appeared now to be frailer. It was a bit like having the joy of being alive but a bit *diffused* in the living of it. Standing, walking, waiting in queues, I felt aged and tired and just wanted to sit down. I was grateful I had not needed chemo. I thanked God for the whole of my life journey and His presence.

In August, I was told that because my tumours had been fed by oestrogen, it was recommended that, for the rest of my life, I take estrogen suppressant tablets. The latest findings had illustrated the helpful benefits of these. Possible side effects were explained, which included, in my case, bone thinning and night-time hot flushes etc. All could be helped with medication. I was reluctant, but even with my history of tumours being slow growing, I was persuaded to start the recommended tablets.

After taking only two tablets, I believed for me, a new assessment would need to be made. I experienced in the night the worst headache I have ever known and the blackest of black despair. There was *no God*, and I felt I wanted to die. I was told to stop taking tablets immediately, and a reassessment for a *different* brand was to be trialled.

I earnestly prayed that night for God's clear answer. 'Please, Father. Tell me yes or no. Should I go forward with this possibly preventative medication?'

I awoke in the darkness, and I heard a clear word resonating. *No!*

Here, as a record of my life, is the decision I made and forwarded to my local GP, cancer surgeon and all who had overseen my breast cancer journey through the years.

The Decision

I have carefully assessed the situation in my life. I have the chance of returning breast cancer in the next few years. This chance is assessed as ' low', but in the case of all *cancer, there is no absolute certainty about anything. It can also come anywhere to anyone. Many safeguards are in place in my life. I am extremely grateful for everyone who has monitored and continues to monitor this.*

I have had a full hysterectomy. This means no ovaries to still charge and produce excess hormones. I have had a third breast operation and five weeks of mop-up radiation. One underarm nodule of 'risk' was removed and came back 'negative'. I am thankful and incredibly grateful.

I also have in place regular ultrasounds and check-ups etc. I have folks to check my eyes, my ears, my skin, and my teeth, a hairdresser, and team to give me a six-weekly maintenance of hair and face. I am years *of age and also have a heart monitor which settles any irregular heartbeats. I feel protected, cosseted, and, on the home front as well,* loved.

I have therefore made a decision. The ongoing suggested tablets of oestrogen suppressants – I know they are valuable, worthwhile with positive outcomes for breast cancer outcomes. There are many, and I know many different options. I started Arimidex (anastrozole)… After taking only a few, I had one dreadful night … violent headache and black, black depression. I even longed for the end of life (maybe not the tablets, some have said . . . but maybe, just maybe, *it was).*

This then caused me to think. Even if there are no side effects or very minor ones, even if the right protection is found, do I really want the added commitment and pressure of this daily tablet taking? (I already take calcium for bone strength support but have always been very grateful not to take anything else . . . It is helpful when health issues arise, i.e. a virus or similar. At least everyone knows it is not a side effect of pills.)

I settled on this question, prayed, and believe last night, I absolutely knew *that my answer must be* no.

The quality of life *is more important to me at this stage of life, even if only minor are the side effects caused by anything that is not necessary to maintaining that life. Weighing up the risks, the protections against this scenario of quality of life . . . prayerfully and absolutely . . . I must say* no *to anything that would disrupt this flow.*

I have made a decision. *I take responsibility for future outcomes.*

***

2018 Comes to an End

Personally, the remainder of 2018 had no remembered highs or lows, rather a coasting at a decidedly more elderly pace. There was, at the *Christmas 2018 season*, for us, a beautiful *at-home* remembrance of Our Lord's birth and also the joy of family connections both before and after the actual day. The fellowship with children and grandchildren is and was always precious in memory.

The summer heat soared, but we looked forward to the new year with faith and His Hope.

[An image sent by a granddaughter – 'Happy New Year!']

CHAPTER 26

2019

Restoration –but a Dark Cloud on the Horizon

The year 2019 was a great year of personal *recovery*. I was still, of course, aging but finding an improvement in aspects of physical strength and mental well-being.

The oncology and abdominal cancer professor to whom I had been referred saw me for my final visit in 2019. It had been five years of regular internal examinations and monitoring.

His report after five years issued to my local doctor said, 'Faye, after five years of careful monitoring, has not shown any warning signs indicative of a secondary spread of breast cancer into her vital organs.'

To me, he said, 'Go and live a long life. You are and have been a source of *joy* to me. *Live healthily and well.*'

He was encouraging, and I was thankfully overwhelmed. I thank God for His race in this area of my life, and I remember others I met on this road, with whom I shared a journey, who did not continue the road but went 'home'.

Our life in 2019 was mostly about care for aging health needs and keeping our Christ life above it *all*. This, for us, was made easier by our life and the raw, natural beauty of our small property, Little 'Char-lee', the small white Maltese/Shih Tzu terrier who now lived with us, contributed to our physical activity and brought lots of joy.

Come on . . . Let's walk.

We made plans in 2020 to undertake the 'Beat It' program designed for seniors to gain strength after various health issues. David was invited because of his diabetes monitoring care plan. He was pre-diabetic but being carefully watched. My heart doctor and both our local doctors and breast cancer Surgeon encouraged us *both* to do this program. A trained physio would work out our routines in a gym facility in a nursing home. We anticipated this 2020 ten-week challenge as being extremely valuable to our life quality.

Towards the end of 2019, our dearly loved first-born child and only daughter's health took a dramatic *dive.* She had led, in recent years, a hectic and very pressurized lifestyle. Her work and home life were extremely stressful and busy. She was mother, wife, and supremely competent in her work life – the personification of the twenty-first-century image of a woman, able to do and accomplish *everything.*

When she first became ill, I was thankful and grateful that her life had slowed down a little. I hoped now for 'time for herself'. However, before Christmas 2019, the situation began to show physical signs of being a much more serious condition.

Once again, summer came with a burst of heat, and we had preparations to make for Christmas celebrations. In separate meetings, we connected with family. We met our three children and five grandchildren. I imagine we *all* knew there was a worrying cloud on the horizon as we farewelled 2019.

CHAPTER 27

2020 Worldwide Pandemic
— A Celebration

Sorrow Cloud

Learning to Live ***Above*** . . . with Christ

The year 2020 witnessed the best and worst of human behaviour, triggered by the worldwide health scare this pandemic brought. Society will argue until proof can be found about how and from where it all emanated. The sadness to me was humanity's response became, in so many ways, indicative of an 'it is all about *me*' attitude to life.

Although Australia was the least effected nation because of our isolation (many other nations, particularly in Europe, became *paralysed* by lockdowns and restrictions), sadly and visibly, the disease, worse than any virus, invaded society and even some churches. A pattern of self-preservation quickly turned into 'my rights'. The enemy of souls drove fear into hearts that even the pursuit of the most basic of human necessities, toilet paper, caused mayhem, anger, and, in some cases, violence. (I do believe in some areas, this was fuelled and driven by a media hungry for a good story.)

One of my lasting memories will be of grown men and women pushing out, in a supermarket, trolley loads of toilet rolls, while people going in to do their normal weekly shop were confronted with bare shelves of all paper-related products. Here in our State of Queensland, this was particularly ridiculous as we had the capacity to make our own toilet rolls, tissues, and all major paper products in our own state.

Personal causes rose with more-than-gentle statements and proclamations. Violence in the streets and open rebellion against safety rules and previously respected laws erupted. 'My *rights*' in all issues – whether it was climate change, sexual persuasions, matters of colour, race, and creed – surfaced and became confrontational during this crisis where millions were dying all around the world.

Only a remnant of God's people had *His* courage to say, 'Keep your focus *above*. What is the destiny of human souls when the mortal body has gone?'

The media could now no longer be trusted to tell the *truth* and *nothing but the truth* in the reporting of events even regarding social and health issues. Long ago, the reporters/journalists I worked with would never compromise on their reporting of events. Now all that seemed to matter was a 'good story' read often by news readers as a true statement but more like a *drama* for public acclaim acted out on a stage. It is all about 'me' – *my* ratings – and to show *my paper or television channel* is the *best*.

The pursuit to find a vaccine to combat COVID-19 became, again, a focus on 'accomplishment' ahead of the possible benefits to help worldwide humanity. Which vaccine? Reports by media were given, usually against the background of scientific, national, and financial interests. Ordinary folk were left with 'which' vaccine and often asked the question 'Why am I being pressured into this important decision before truthful and full information is given to *all* specialists with advice that is consistent, identical, and helpful?'

Anti-vac extremists then flooded media sources, and for a period in 2020, many here were thankful to wait until the hype settled. Sadly, in 2021, the search for this health truth remains blurred.

One intrinsic *truth* remains, however. We may save this mortal body, but one day it will *perish.* 'Where will the soul travel when the body has decayed?' This was my childhood question. Praise God that as 2020 continued, this was the reality of my personal *truth* which unfolded in life. This continued to be revealed as 'Keep looking upwards but ever learning about.'

An Old Rugged Cross

Humanity's immortal soul destiny is secure in 2020 only because the River of Redemption Blood still flows. Sinful humanity can never save themselves. There is repentance and accepting Jesus Christ as the *one* Saviour *for every mortal everywhere.*

Thus continues my 2020 journey to find *who He really is.* This incredible year continues with the celebration of *fifty years* of married life.

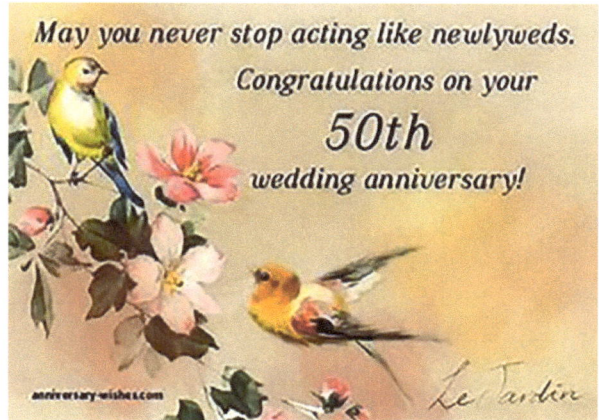

This was a special and unexpected celebration at the Aglow meeting. Although under COVID guidelines, we were few in number, the surprise and joy of this time with Aglow family remains a special memory. Thank you to the great friends and thanks to God for our love and life in *Him*.

Hamilton Island, 15–21 November 2020

Our plans to go to Fiji as part of our celebration of *fifty years* together could not eventuate because of COVID. Even the conference we had hoped to attend while there was cancelled. We were advised, when our holiday money was returned, that our airline tickets could be transferred to a Queensland destination.

For us, this became a God-blessed time together. We went to Hamilton Island – one of the Whitsunday group of Pacific Islands. These are *part of the State of Queensland* and, as such, were in COVID lockdown, the same as the mainland. We were privileged to be able to go with full attention and service given to us but with a lack of thousands of visitors. We experienced island life where even birds returned to settle in vast numbers.

The airport processing in Brisbane was also a wonderful experience. Practically deserted, with all usual milling around pushing and shoving absent, it was instead a delightful stroll. Our cases and custom clearance – with my involved pacemaker scanning and COVID distancing, temperature checks, etc. – flowed with speed and efficiency. We arrived in the departure lounge, relaxed, and excitedly anticipated our flight and the days ahead. *It was a special time.*

Interaction with island folk, who were now in responsible positions because of overseas staff not returning, helped me understand how important COVID lockdown safety was for them – for us also. It was about health and safety but a joyous return to a more peaceful and less 'touristy' way of life for everyone.

We thank God that in the 'midst' of world crisis, we had a blessed six days.

Our first view from the Reef View Hotel balcony, 15/11/20.

The sixteenth – one visitor came in the early morning. Soon, there were two.

We had many visitors on our last morning, the twenty-first.

Multiplication

God spoke to me about multiplication with these birds. I will therefore keep a separate chapter for the actual anniversary, *17 October*, and conclude this chapter with gratitude for this part of my life and give background information.

Regarding the birds, on our first morning, I met the first white Major Mitchell cockatoo. I gave thanks and welcomed him. Then there were two, and day by day, more came. On our last morning, they kept coming in a constant display of joy. Faith has assured me that this is like God's blessings. Let's always give thanks for the small, and He will multiply. This applies to His comfort in the valleys as well as the great joy on the heights.

Hamilton days began with a peaceful feeling of holiday. Breakfast

168

came with room service. We made a choice to eat at the inside table or sit on the balcony and bask in the view of blue Pacific water and the Whitsunday Islands. We enjoyed it when sailing craft with different coloured sails and decks came for instruction lessons or racing displays.

We went out exploring and walking and usually had meals out. Fish locally caught and chips was a favourite. We met with a couple of young people who rejoiced with us that the Queensland border had been shut. At least now the COVID threat was no longer a certainty for them and their families. On a couple of occasions, we enjoyed bringing home meals and relaxing on the comfortable balcony chairs.

We visited the beautiful chapel nestled into the hillside and remembered the good Samaritans who miraculously arrived after our time of reflection and prayer there and drove us back to our hotel. (I had been overconfident, in the heat, of my ability to walk back down the steep hill. There was no return bus after we exited at the top, and we had walked down to the chapel and stopped and stayed there for a time.)

I knew I was *exhausted* and sat down on a grassy slope. The young couple were as surprised to see us as we were them. It was a *God moment* of sharing and faith. Everywhere on Hamilton we went, we met with kindness and enthusiasm for life from the young island folk and often tourists like us where we shared our experiences.

The day before our anniversary, we were sitting beside the hotel pool when we were surprised by a young waiter with a tray of nibbles and two glasses of champagne.

'Happy fiftieth wedding anniversary to our guests by the pool!' called out the Manager, and we, who had slipped out for a quick dip, became the focus of attention.

Gratitude and thanksgiving for the memories!

CHAPTER 27B

2020 — COVID and Fiftieth Wedding Anniversary

A Cloud on the Personal Horizon

Whitehaven Beach, Whitsunday Island — A Brief Visit, a Lifetime Memory

17 October 2020

T he day began with an enjoyable relaxed breakfast, again with a morning of warm, brilliant sunshine and our stunning view across the pristine, clear blue water. David had been able to get a booking for a cruise around the islands. Because of COVID and closed borders, this also was a relaxed and less pressured outing. Even with less-than-usual close contact with others, there was lots of laughter, and the journey was laidback and picture perfect.

We disembarked at Whitehaven Beach, where the couple of hours there was time for a swim and picnic. I wanted more than anything to sit in the gently flowing, rippling water on the dazzling white sand and be grateful for life and the beauty around. The dazzling white sand on this beach is unique in the world. It is pure silica and, even on the most scorching day, will not burn feet and is even perfect for cleaning or polishing jewellery. My wedding ring returned home shining like brand new.

I felt confident as I traversed the wide beach and slid down a gentle slope and flopped into the water. I had an enjoyable few minutes lying there, letting the ebb and flow of the water wash over me. It was great until I thought it was time to leave, to join David under the tree. *I could not get up!* The grip of sand and tide prevented me from gaining a foothold, and aging, stiff knees stopped me from powering into a standing position.

I heaved myself backwards up the sandy incline and then called to David, who had to haul me up like a beached whale and steady me back across the beach, where I plopped, exhausted, on my towel. I had enjoyed the swim but was reminded again that age does have limiting intrusions, even on peaceful island life.

It was a lovely cruise back to our departure terminal and a brief time when we returned to the hotel for a cuppa and a rest. Then it was time for dinner – a special celebratory meal downstairs in our hotel, beside the pool.

'Happy Anniversary – Faye and David.'
Hotel dining room – beside the pool.

It was a private corner – but we were not alone! A wonderful meal, a wonderful day – we give thanks for our fifty years together.

5 December 2020

David organised a special pre-Christmas lunch.

It was wonderful to have everyone together – us, our three children, and their spouses and children. Now it is indeed a priceless memory saved as a picture but stored in our hearts *forever*.

I can't finish the 2020 section of *Shafts* without mention of my spiritual heartache at how the world was suffering in lockdowns and COVID restrictions and desiring that, in some way, I could express God's love for His people despite their seemingly mass disregard for *Him*. Workbook Press contacted me about producing a small book of Christian meditations, and this little book was featured in the *Manila Bookfair*. My hope and prayer was that butterflies would fly into the hands of all who needed gentle encouragement. I have no idea if it achieved its purpose, but my heart in 2020 was encouraged as I saw the cover and remembered what God alone did with butterflies in 2011.

For all who have suffered in this crisis year, I offer up a *prayer*.

May the God of hope *touch human hearts and restore in them their full worth so the* one *who came to save their* souls *can (with the assistance of a safe vaccine) restore the world to a place where fear is conquered and His* kingdom *will* come.

In Jesus's name. Amen.

CHAPTER 28

2021

Disturbances – Vision – Personal Grief

Despite hopes of a better year than *the COVID year* 2020, 2021 begins with a very disturbed worldwide realization that this pandemic would not simply go away and life return to humanity's expectations of a normal, self-focussed life. Sadly, even more violence invaded our streets as various causes and social issues vied for attention. '*It's all about me!* My culture, my rights, my thwarted desires, etc.' Then there was an increasing awareness that the vaccine was not the whole solution. Issues were much deeper.

In the early months, my personal life was disrupted by an increasing number of publishing houses wanting to republish my books – all out there 'online'. Every suggestion required financial commitment from me. I simply could *not* comply. I had no money.

I had given up 'except in God's timing' any thought of God's writing gift somehow helping our financial life as we age. Any royalties were such a pittance, they vanished in the increasing cost of later-life living. I could continue to write simply as a voice in the world through the maintenance of websites and blogging. I thank God for this.

One phone voice from *New York* rang with a depth of truth, and her inspiration has fuelled in me the desire to keep writing in 2021 in the middle of *all* which unfolded. Even if what she said is but marshmallows on a bench, if she phones back in December, I am prepared to talk again. Her inspiration fuelled in me a new writing goal which I never would have undertaken. I never wanted to write about 'myself'. I began *Shafts of Gold*, which is about God, not about my personal genetics etc. It is about learning of the *one I wanted to know*.

After prayer, I believe He confirmed in my heart, *'Do it.'* The 2021 writing journey, therefore, has been to finish *Shafts*. He has led me, reminded me, and inspired me. This, now at the end of July, will probably complete not my/our lives but the 'shafts of gold' search for who

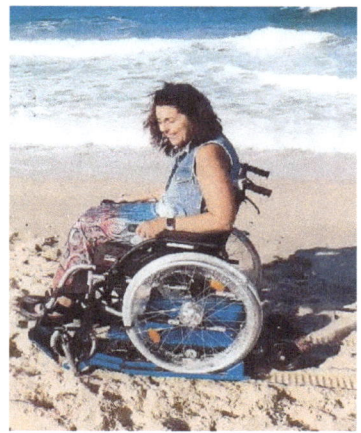

God is. I know how much there is still to learn, and this must ever, like a little child, be the way I continue to live.

Our daughter's decline was becoming obvious, but our memories of late 2020 are of her in her motorised wheelchair, loving the sea and the wind in her hair, powering along the sand.

The 2021 year was to be the final in the life of our first-born child – a shaft of gold on the day of her birth I recorded as *a God blessing* – and this, she continued to be all the days of her life.

In early March, we could see the ravages of motor neurone disease becoming more obvious, and as her parents, we prayed and grieved. *I would like to express appreciation to the wonderful carers and rallying family and friends who made her final weeks full of beautiful memories.*

Alison's birthday on 23 May 2021 at Woodgate Beach will be remembered by us all as a happy memory. Her smile energised her spirit, which radiated her appreciation for family and life.

For my birthday in June, a beautiful pre-prepared card in Alison's handwriting with flowers and chocolates arrived. It had been bought under her instructions, by carers, and was delivered to me at home. David brought it back with him after a father/daughter visit to Alison in her Childers home.

Sadly, we would never visit her in her home again. She was admitted to palliative care, Bundaberg Hospital, in early July. Son-in-law Mark phoned to advise us and her family – i.e. brothers, uncle, and cousins – her time was short. Alison made her decision not to allow her life to be prolonged by artificial means. She desired to breathe on her own and only be assisted to do this peacefully.

David and I prayed as we set forth with our little terrier Char-lee for the three-hour drive to see our daughter for what we knew was to say *goodbye.* The hospital staff and nurses in this Palliative Care Unit will be remembered by me with gratitude always for their excellent care and loving help and understanding.

The peace of God permeated the whole unit, and even the little dog was affected. When they welcomed her to come in and 'stay' for our visit, she adapted to the circumstances in an amazing way. Our feisty, barking, very excitable little dog became a loving addition to the gathering.

One of the male nurses commented later, 'She would be an excellent care dog in units of high-level needs.'

Thank you, little one.

Peace was a swamping reality, and I knew there was one last thing I had to do to say goodbye to this beloved child who came as a God gift in our lives. I placed a butterfly on her chest and took her hand. I thanked her for years of love she had always lavished on us.

Then I whispered, 'I now, with faith, cut the spiritual cord which has always joined us since your birth.' I made a physical action of scissors and said, 'May your spirit now soar to be with His Spirit into eternity.'

I kissed her. I sensed her breathing change. Inside me, I knew a wrenching pain of loss. I had no idea why I had done what I did but *knew* it was of God. Mark's mother held me tightly as now, carrying the little dog, I went to sit in the garden. David then prayed and farewelled his child. I heard later his prayer was a great blessing for all who heard both his prayer and benediction.

We journeyed home and, in the next few days, waited to hear of her passing. She surprised all medical people, family, and friends by continuing to breathe until the following Wednesday the twenty-first.

Only God knows what He wanted to do in the lives of us all as she continued to breathe. Peace was maintained in her care, and I believe all who were *spiritually minded* understood the Biblical precept that God gives breath and only God should be allowed to take it away.

Breath

Alison Vera Burns né Roots breathed first on 23 May 1972. Her final breath was made on 21 July 2021. *Deo gracious!*

Personally, I knew without the p*resence* of this God I had searched my whole to find, in *His* fullness, I would sink. Alison's loss was significant because her *love* had always sustained and supported us as humans, and through the years, we treasured her many kindnesses to us as parents.

When you know the reality, as if a huge chunk of your life has been removed from your view, grief can be intense. Only a *big God* can minister His peace, His love, and His strength in joy, as He did in the following days. Peace was with us both, *deep, abiding peace.* I even found this extraordinary *peace* as I continued to write and *blog*.

I shared *grief* as a testimony of faith to others. It was, for me, however, a profound and deeply moving experience. On *Shafts*, I admit I needed supernatural enabling as the *wave* was forceful and I woke up in tears. I went back to sleep, and the rest flowed. It is simply expressed – the truth – but even on that lonely strip of sand before I looked up, absolute hopelessness was my 'feeling'.

Grief

Like a mighty ocean wave, grief swamped me. Two words – '*Never again! Never again!*' – pounded in the sea. I cried for what is gone and never will be again. I grieved for the loss of our beloved daughter. The sorrow was intense, yet I knew, – somehow, I knew – I had to ride the wave to shore.

I landed on the sand.

Look up!

With me.. The two words resonated on the wind.

I was left alone on the sand.

'Now,' the voice in my spirit said, '*Stand*. Walk on . . . I am with you.'

I now walk along this beach of my life, and though I grieve . . . I know the wave of my grieving will always carry me back to shore and keep me looking up where He sees from on high, where she is with Him yet lives with me through His Spirit down here.

Thank You, Lord! *Amen*.

Alison's Memorial Legacy

Alison's legacy was revealed in the beauty of the Service of remembrance held in the funeral chapel in Bundaberg on 28 July 2021. It had been planned by Alison herself. She chose the format and the readings and even wrote her own eulogy, read and recorded by a career. A huge photo of our daughter was on an overhead screen.

Her words of gratitude for what she had seen and done in her life resonated. She expressed appreciation and love for all family, friends, work colleagues, and wonderful health providers. While photos were passing on the screen, we saw her life as a tapestry of events and appreciated afresh her passion for life and for others.

The Service was *life affirming* in every way. *Her dad, with passion and faith, read the twenty-third psalm.*

The pastor and his wife had known the family for many years since their children had been in preschool. He passionately wove the music, the scriptures, and the *eulogy* together in a wonderful address where he affirmed the service was a legacy from her and should be remembered as being about the power of *love, family, faith, and forgiveness.*

It was only later, I could clearly understand, that the contemporary music Al had chosen, woven into her life – surrounded by many loved ones who had little or no faith – would speak into their lives. Celine Dion's song 'Ashes', playing as her coffin was carried out, shocked as well as brought us all to tears. I heard the final words clearly.

Can beauty rise from ashes when love *is there?*

Absolutely! The Christian response. Amen.

The three song choices included 'Run to You' (not a capital Y on the song jacket but made a capital Y by Alison). 'Oceans' was about her love of the sea but also spoke of the Creator, and the final, 'Ashes', will be understood by everyone if they listen to the full track. Her scripture choices were all about the certainty of destination when the *Saviour* is followed.

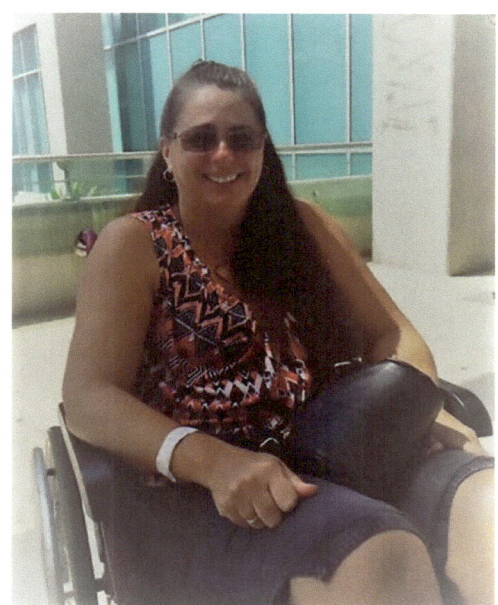

Memories and love will last until we meet
again. *A new day will dawn. Amen!*

Alison with Her Family
Beach — JUNE 2020
Memories . . . live on.

CHAPTER 29

Hard To Write

The Endeavour to Complete an Understanding of
the Complex Searchings of My Life's Journey

A little girl wanted spiritual answers

The old lady tries to explain the answers life has shown.

This then is the final shaft of gold in this life discovery of an *awesome God.*

Remembering all the *shafts of gold* in my life and *all* the God-directed influences, I can only gaze heavenwards and give *thanks.* So many of the twists and the seemingly unimportant, now I can see as profound, humbling, and mind-numbingly 'awe-inspiring'.

I know *He is real.* Now I understand I will never really *know* the *fullness* of *who* He is. He is more *holy*, *righteous*, and beyond what, in this *natural realm*, my human mind could – even with divine assistance – ever grasp. The final realization lies beyond this life . . . in eternity.

These then are my final conclusions based only upon my personal life and confirmed by the *written word.* He is in and through the very fabric of human existence, revealed as Jesus Christ in human body yet ever in *His Spirit.*

Father, Son, and Spirit one divine entity. Nothing is *impossible! He* is beyond and in and through it *all* – the *whole universe.* He is *divine love, divine spirit. Eternity* is in His hands

Jesus had to come if divine love was to be fulfilled. The whole Bible as a handbook reveals the reason of all things pertaining to *redemption* and mere mortals being *saved* from their sinful natures to bring them to an incredibly *holy God* We must live according to His holy rules in our modern day, living under a covering of *grace* with a free will to follow or decline. *Love* must be our desire in everything we do – not *self-focussed* but God directed and focussed, love by His prescribed order and rules . . . all the days we live.

The Book of Job teaches us that through extreme sorrow, loss, heartache, and confusion, he could say, 'My Redeemer lives!' Although in dust, ashes, and totally broken, this was his testimony. The personal loss of our first-born after her being a comfort in our lives for forty-nine years brought me to a *reality* of who God is and has given me the ability to write this last *Shafts* chapter. I pray as I do that if this memoir comes to encourage others to keep *seeking*, keep *looking upwards,* then it was for a purpose. I had to write it down. *He inspired!*

The prophet Nehemiah, so long ago, saw death and destruction all around him. He recorded – *'Not by might not by power but by my Spirit,' said the Lord.*

In His Spirit, in these *grace* years since Christ died to set mankind *free,* we must walk on to stand and live *triumphantly*. My personal testimony in this final chapter must be that *peace beyond comprehension* has been His gift during Alison's final days. Her death has proven this to me absolutely. Thank you to all the folk who prayed. God heard your prayers.

There was *joy inexplicable* – not external or with laughter but an internal bubble. I was amazed how images I saw of two birds doing a soft-shoe shuffle, and two laughing sheep came to me as God gifts, and this bubble kept my day flowing. 'The joy of the Lord is my strength' became my *truth*.

I believe that as a blood-bought adopted child of God – My Father in heaven, who is *spirit* – all of the realm of angels, visions, dreams, and divine comfort are my inheritance and are there for *all* of His redeemed children according to His will and for His purpose. I thank *Him*.

- *He is absolute holiness.*
- To all of humanity – frail, sin-natured, selfish, and tiny – He is *Saviour* if accepted.
- In human likeness, He said, *'I am the way … Follow Me."*
- *Water, sacrificial, lives lived unto Him. Then the Spirit will be empowered.*

For All He Can Then Be — The God of the Impossible

I conclude with thanks to all who love and have loved me on my journeys, and I pay tribute to the non-humans who either chose to live with us or were rescued or chosen by us. These are the animals of Chynoweth. Each one brought and brings love and comfort. *Thank you all* – Penny, Frosty, Bobby, Tarsha, Megs, Chessa, Gemmy, Frangi, Shaggy, Kel, and with us *now* . . . Charlee.

Ahead, who knows? Only one.

189

INDEX

Gympie Hospital 134